DEMOCRATIZATION AND ETHNIC NATIONALISM: AFRICAN AND EASTERN EUROPEAN EXPERIENCES

POLICY ESSAY NO.14

DEMOCRATIZATION AND ETHNIC NATIONALISM: AFRICAN AND EASTERN EUROPEAN EXPERIENCES

MARINA OTTAWAY

OVERSEAS DEVELOPMENT COUNCIL
WASHINGTON, DC

Copyright © 1994 by Overseas Development Council, Washington, DC

Library of Congress Cataloging-In-Publication Data

Ottaway, Marina.
   Democratization and ethnic nationalism: African and Eastern European experiences/Marina Ottaway.

Policy Essay No. 14
Includes bibliographical references.
   1. Europe, Eastern—Politics and government—1989–   2. Africa, Sub-Saharan—Politics and government—1960–   3. Democracy—Europe, Eastern.   4. Democracy—Africa, Sub-Saharan.   5. Nationalism—Europe, Eastern.   6. Nationalism—Africa, Sub-Saharan.   7. Europe, Eastern—Ethnic relations.   8. Africa, Sub-Saharan—Ethnic relations. I. Title.   II. Series.

DJK51.O89   1994   320.5'4'09049—dc20   94-36131 CIP

ISBN: 1-56517-019-9

Printed in the United States of America.

Director of Publications: Christine E. Contee
Publications Editor: Jacqueline Edlund-Braun
Edited by Kathleen Lynch
Cover design: Snoreck Design Group
Book design: Tim Kenney Design Partners, Inc.

The views expressed in this volume are those of the author and do not necessarily represent those of the Overseas Development Council as an organization or of its individual officers or Board, Council, Program Advisory Group, and staff members.

Contents

Foreword

A resurgence of ethnic nationalism around the world is one of the most unexpected and tragic characteristics of our times. This explosion of nationalism threatens hoped-for transition to democracy that was expected to follow with the end of the Cold War. As Marina Ottaway points out in this *Policy Essay*, nationalist regimes are seldom democratic. Rather, this ideology tends to put the interests of the many ahead of those of the individual and provides a justification for government curbs on civil and political rights.

In multi-ethnic countries, political liberalization is too frequently a prelude to ethnic conflict. This raises difficult questions about the relationship between democratization and ethnic conflict. For the United States, which has set promoting democratization as a major foreign policy objective, understanding the relationship is critical. Is it possible that by promoting the political opening necessary for a democratic transition, the United States may be contributing to intensified ethnic strife?

Marina Ottaway's analysis of the early phases of the democratization process and the appearance of militant ethnic nationalism in the former Yugoslavia, the former Czechoslovakia, South Africa, and Ethiopia finds no causal link between the two processes. She does conclude, however, that in all cases the opening acted as a catalyst that made an existing ethnic problem much more acute. Governments and the international community must make efforts to manage such nationalism in ways that are compatible with democracy an integral part of any attempt to promote political reform in multi-ethnic societies.

ODC was fortunate to have Marina Ottaway, who is a professor at Georgetown University, as the 1993–94 Davidson Sommers Fellow. Her work on ethnic nationalism and democratization is groundbreaking and will make an important contribution to an issue that absolutely requires the attention of policymakers.

The Overseas Development Council gratefully acknowledges The Ford Foundation and The Rockefeller Foundation for their support of the Council's overall program and The Equitable Life Assurance Society of the United States for its support the Davidson Sommers Fellowship on International Development Studies, which made possible Dr. Ottaway's research and the publication of this *Policy Essay*.

John W. Sewell
President
October 1994

Acknowledgments

It is impossible for me to mention individually all those who have contributed to this work. I am particularly thankful to the many in the United States, Yugoslavia, and Slovakia who have shown great patience in helping an Africanist navigate the troubled waters of Eastern European politics.

My research assistant, Heidi Brooks, was enormously helpful in tracking down the documents I asked for and calling to my attention others I was in danger of overlooking.

The essay greatly benefited from the comments offered by Michael Chege, Christine Contee, Catherine Gwin, Allen Kassof, William Maynes, William Pfaff, Crawford Young, and William Zartman. I want to thank them for offering their insights.

Executive Summary

Promoting democracy around the world is a major goal of U.S. foreign policy in the post-Cold War era. But many countries that started a transition from authoritarianism to democracy have seen the process threatened, and in some cases derailed, by a sudden explosion of ethnic nationalism. Democratic openings, as this study shows, do not cause ethnic nationalism. In all cases, the conflicts were brewing earlier, but they were kept in check by the authoritarian governments. The removal of these governments created space not only for democratic forces to develop, but for ethnic conflicts to escalate.

The disintegration of the Soviet empire and the partition of Yugoslavia and Czechoslovakia provide dramatic examples of the renewed strength of ethnic nationalism in Eastern Europe. Less noticed but equally important is the problem in Africa. As competitive elections are held in an increasing number of countries, new political parties emerge that draw their support from specific ethnic groups. This in turn can lead to an increase in the level of ethnic conflict in all its manifestations, from communal strife to ethnic cleansing.

Ethnic nationalism, the events of the early 1990s show, creates its own vicious circle. It led to the partition of the Soviet Union and Yugoslavia and it is now threatening the new states as well. From Central Asia to Eastern Europe, the new states formed after the fall of communism are themselves threatened by ethnic conflict. If unchecked, this vicious circle threatens the future of democracy, which only a few years ago appeared to be very bright.

The countries discussed in this study—Yugoslavia (and after the partition Croatia), Czechoslovakia (and after the partition Slovakia), South Africa, and Ethiopia—illustrate how a perverse relation between democracy and ethnic conflict can complicate or even derail progress toward democracy and highlight some of the problems that need to be addressed to make democracy possible in multi-ethnic societies.

Yugoslavia shows how democratization can increase the strength of conflicting nationalisms, but also how the partition of a country does not constitute a solution. The nationalism that led Croatia to secede was a threat to the rights of the Serbian minority within the borders of the new country. Serbian nationalism in turn constituted a threat to the territorial integrity of the new Croat state. The resulting civil war was a major set-back for democracy. Resuming democratization will require not only negotiating the end to the hostilities, but also devising a political system that recognizes the rights, and thus allays the fears, of all minorities.

Czechoslovakia's experience is similar to Yugoslavia in some respects, but it also contains a more encouraging lesson. In Czechoslovakia, too, democratization fanned the flames of ethnic conflict, leading to the partition of the country into Slovakia and the Czech Republic. And in Slovakia, as in Croatia, the nationalism of the majority heightened the fears, and thus the nationalism, of the minorities, in particular the Hungarians. But Slovakia has avoided civil war and may be able to work out a compromise solution by adhering to the principles set forth by the Council of Europe and the Conference for Security and Cooperation in Europe (CSCE). Slovakia thus highlights how internationally recognized principles concerning ethnic relations can help contain conflict.

In South Africa, democratization meant moving away from the apartheid system, which was based not only on racial segregation but also on an attempt to divide the black majority by inciting the nationalism of the various ethnic groups. Nevertheless, the political opening that followed the unbanning of the African National Congress in 1990 also led to an explosion of ethnic nationalism, particularly among Zulus and Afrikaners. This nationalism threatened the success of the first universal suffrage elections of April 1994. A last minute agreement among the incumbent white government, the African National Congress, and the Zulu Inkatha Freedom Party saved the elections, but it also embedded the recognition of ethnicity into the South African political system. While it is too early to talk about the success of democracy in South Africa, the experience so far suggests that democratization in multi-ethnic societies requires not the suppression of ethnic identities, but their accommodation in the political system.

Finally Ethiopia approached the problem of ethnic nationalism in a way that made it impossible to pursue democracy without leading to the disintegration of the country. The new government that came to power in 1991 professed adherence to democracy, but it tried to solve the problem of ethnic nationalism by following the old Soviet model, which had also guided Yugoslavia and Czechoslovakia under the socialist regimes. The Ethiopian government divided the country into ethnic regions nominally enjoying a degree of autonomy, but it also sought to maintain centralized control by curbing the activity of independent political parties. The evidence from the former socialist countries shows that such a system can maintain unity and contain ethnic conflict only as long as the center remains strong and repressive. Disintegration results when the center weakens during a political opening. The system chosen thus appeared to condemn Ethiopia to continued authoritarianism or to disintegration. Ethiopia offered a lesson on how ethnic conflict should *not* be managed by countries pursuing democratization.

To the United States, which is trying to promote democracy, the revival of ethnic nationalism presents a considerable challenge. Ethnic nationalism is stimulated by political openings, but it can halt further progress toward democracy and cause high levels of violence and dramatic violations of human rights. Yet democracy is the only system that provides a hope that ethnic conflicts can be managed successfully. The problem is how to encourage democratic systems that take into account the particular problems of multi-ethnic societies.

So far the United States has not recognized clearly enough that multi-ethnic countries, particularly those with a history of acute ethnic conflict, cannot embrace democracy without simultaneously tackling the problem of ethnic nationalism. Efforts to manage such nationalism in ways compatible with democracy must become an integral part of any attempt to promote political reform in multi-ethnic societies.

U.S. policy needs to take into consideration the different circumstances of Africa and Europe. European institutions have recognized that democracy in multi-ethnic countries presents special challenges and have elaborated principles and guidelines that can help countries manage ethnic nationalism. African countries remain reluctant to accept that at least some demands by ethnic groups are legitimate and that, in any case, efforts to outlaw ethnic nationalism are futile. As a result, they have not devised mechanisms to guide democratizing countries as they try to cope with the challenge of ethnicity. The United States thus needs to push European countries to implement the principles to which they have agreed in theory and to help African countries to adopt a realistic set of guidelines to manage ethnic nationalism before it leads to an acute crisis.

In the last few years European countries and institutions such as the CSCE have approved numerous documents concerning the rights of ethnic groups, particularly the more vulnerable minorities. In so doing, they have come to the conclusion that the defense of individual rights, which is crucial in any democratic system, is not by itself sufficient to safeguard minorities, and that some group rights must be protected as well—rights to local autonomy or use of the mother language, for example. If implemented, these principles could defuse ethnic conflict. The United States must push countries to adhere to these principles by making it clear that governments that discriminate against ethnic minorities, or do not recognize their special rights, cannot be considered democratic and that this will affect their relations with the United States. But ethnic minorities also need to be told that their demands will only be recognized as legitimate when they fall within the realm of internationally recognized principles.

Africa poses a different challenge. As a first step it needs to develop a more realistic attitude toward ethnic nationalism. The United States must help African countries and institutions acknowledge the inevitability of ethnic tensions and devise principles to help contain and manage them in a democratic framework. Such principles need to be developed by Africans on the basis of the conditions their countries face and cannot simply be a transposition of European tenets. As Europe illustrates, the acceptance of general guidelines does not guarantee implementation in the specific cases. Nevertheless, such general principles are important, and African countries need to be encouraged to develop them.

The case studies examined in this book show that democratization and ethnic nationalism have emerged as two aspects of the same process of political transformation during the 1990s. The United States has emphasized democratization without paying sufficient attention to the management of ethnic nationalism. But the outbreak of ethnic nationalism can bring the process of democratization to a halt. It is thus imperative that the problem receive more attention by policymakers interested in promoting democracy.

Part I.

Introduction

NATIONALISM AND ETHNIC NATIONALISM

■ DURING THE 1990S, NATIONALISM HAS EMERGED once again as a major ideological force, a threat to the stability and the territorial integrity of a large number of states, and an obstacle to democratic transformation everywhere. The hope that the defeat of socialism would mean the triumph of democracy has proven overly optimistic. In many countries, nationalism has already shown itself to be not only a powerful force, but also a profoundly antidemocratic one.

Because nationalism has many meanings and many historical variants, some clarifications are needed at the outset. Nationalism can be ethnic or non-ethnic, democratic or authoritarian, divisive or unifying. In nineteenth century Europe, where it first appeared as a major political force, nationalism was ethnic, although the term was not used. The essence of nationalism was the belief that there existed natural, ethnic, or national communities, characterized by a common culture, language, and history, and that these natural communities had the right to organize themselves as states. The nationalism of the fascist regimes of the 1930s was also ethnic, based on the concept of the national community, the *volk*. In contrast, the nationalism of the independence struggle in the colonies was not ethnic. In Africa, nationalist leaders were not agitating for the right of particular national or ethnic groups to form their own states, but for those of colonized peoples to independence. They accepted the colonies carved by Europe without regard to ethnic and historical boundaries as the basis for the new independent states, and they were convinced that in time the citizens of each country would develop a common sense of nationhood. In Europe, nationalism meant that the nation would organize as a state, in Africa that the state would create a nation.

Nationalism was a unifying force in parts of Europe during the nineteenth century, above all in Italy and Germany where a plethora of small political entities was pulled together in the name of the nation. Nationalism was also a unifying force in Africa in the early post-colonial period. But nationalism has also proven to be a force of disintegration, for example in the destruction of the Austro-Hungarian and Ottoman empires.

The nationalism of the 1990s is a divisive force. This is most evident in Eastern Europe and the former Soviet Union, where nationalism has already led to the fragmentation of many states. In Africa, unambiguously secessionist movements are still rare, but nationalism is increasingly concerned with the rights of pre-existing nations or ethnic groups to recognition and autonomy, rather than with the creation of new nations out of disparate populations.

Around the world, nationalism today means ethnic nationalism, as it did in nineteenth century Europe. Once again, the national or ethnic community is taken as the foundation on which a state should be built. Whether such communities can really be defined on the basis of objective criteria is much less important than the fact they have chosen a certain identity and act accordingly. A discussion of whether Bosnian Muslims can legitimately be defined as an ethnic group does not add to the understanding of the politics of Bosnia or help devise a solution.

Historically, nationalism can be both a part of the process of democratic transformation and an obstacle to it. In the nineteenth century, nationalism was by and large a democratic force, whereas the nationalism of the nazi and fascist regimes was deeply anti-democratic. At present, nationalism appears to be a force inimical to democracy. In several Eastern European countries, for example, the old socialist elites are returning to power under a new nationalist facade. And nationalist organizations in South Africa tried to derail the elections of April 1994 that marked the transition from apartheid.

. . . .

THE NEW WAVE OF ETHNIC NATIONALISM

■ THE NEW WAVE OF ETHNIC NATIONALISM has already engulfed the successor states of the former Soviet Union, Yugoslavia, and Czechoslovakia and is threatening the stability of virtually all Eastern European and Balkan countries. Ethnic nationalism appears to be on the increase in Africa as well. The slaughter in Burundi in late 1993 and Rwanda a few months later, or the marching of Zulu *impis*, brandishing so-called traditional weapons in the streets of Johannesburg, have attracted attention. But ethnic conflict is becoming a more visible problem in many other countries, including in some supposedly undergoing a democratic transformation. Perhaps more important, ethnic nationalism in Africa is no longer automatically dismissed as "tribalism," a sign of underdevelopment that time and modernization will cure. Rather, openly ethnic nationalist movements have arisen in many countries, advocating separation or at least autonomy for various peoples and challenging the most basic principle adhered to by African states: the inviolability of colonial borders. If unchecked, these movements could lead to the long-dreaded opening of the Pandora's box of border changes.

There are no regions of the world that are not affected to some degree by this wave of ethnic nationalism. Even the democratic, industrialized countries are challenged by a revival of ethnic and regional identities. The United States itself is facing demands for bilingualism and Afrocentric education in its schools, a rejection on principle of the melting pot ideal of merging separate ethnic and national cultures in one single American identity. Such trends do not doom democracy, but they challenge the notion that democracy requires equal rights for all, but not the recognition of the special rights of minorities.

The possibility that ethnic nationalism will lead to the break-up of some states is not a problem in itself. Borders have never been eternal, and there is no reason to assume that present ones are different, although they were frozen in place for almost a half century by the Cold War. The consequences of a reconfiguration of states in itself need not be tragic, but the present wave of nationalism is creating a vicious circle. An ethnic group that has fought for its separate state and won all too often disregards the rights of its own minorities, who then feel threatened and become nationalistic in turn. Nationalism caused Croatia to declare its independence, but then led the Serbian minority in Croatia to declare its own independent republic in the Krajina; it led to a peaceful split between the Czech Republic and Slovakia, but also created the threat of a clash between a nationalistic Slovak government and an increasingly mobilized Hungarian minority. The threat of chaos and violence increases as conflicting nationalisms incite each other.

Ethnic conflict is not a new development. Studies have concluded that it has been escalating steadily, at least since the 1950s.[1] It is now becoming a destabilizing force not only in the affected states but also internationally. As a consequence, it can no longer be treated as an internal problem of sovereign states in whose domestic affairs the international community should not interfere.

The explosion of nationalism also threatens the transition from authoritarianism that was the expected peace dividend of the end of the Cold War. The United States, particularly under the Clinton administration, has made the spread of democracy into a major goal of its foreign policy. But new, nationalist regimes are seldom democratic. Nationalism is a collective ideology, putting the interests of the collectivity ahead of those of the individual. This provides a justification for government curbs on civil and political rights—dissident ideas are seen by nationalist regimes as a betrayal of the nation, just as they were seen as a betrayal of the working class by communist regimes. Furthermore, no matter what ideology they claim to adhere to, regimes threatened by militant nationalist movements are unlikely to pursue democratic reforms.

Ethnic nationalism frequently appears in multi-ethnic countries following a political opening that was expected to lead to a democratic transition. This raises the troublesome question whether there is a causal link between the beginning of democratization and the explosion of nationalism in countries with a multi-ethnic population. This is not a theoretical issue. Promoting democratization is a major goal of U.S. foreign policy, but if the political opening necessary for a democratic transition increases ethnic conflict, the United States may end by contributing to civil war rather than democracy.

In an attempt to clarify the issue, this study analyzes relations between the early phases of a democratization process and the appearance of militant ethnic nationalism in four cases. Two are Eastern European countries that disintegrated under the impact of ethnic nationalist demands—the former Yugoslavia and the former Czechoslovakia. At least some of their successor states are also threatened by new nationalist movements. The other two are African countries where ethnic nationalism is threatening democratization—South Africa and Ethiopia. In both African cases, nationalist organizations are openly seeking recognition of ethnicity as the only legitimate principle of state formation, a new point of view in Africa, that if accepted could threaten all states.

Ethnic nationalism is not yet as widespread a problem in Africa as it is in Eastern Europe and in the Soviet successor states. But the example of these parts of the world is influencing African movements, in particular providing justification for the claim that ethnic nationalism is a legitimate force well accepted by the international community. It is because of the demonstration effect of post-socialist nationalism on Africa that this study includes examples from both Eastern Europe and Africa. Soviet successor states were not included to keep the essay within manageable proportions.

The analysis of these four countries that experienced a political opening and simultaneously an increase in ethnic conflict reveals no simple causal link between the two. However, in all cases, the opening acted as a catalyst that made an existing ethnic problem much more acute.

The response of the United States and other members of the international community to the wave of ethnic nationalism has so far been inadequate and above all ad hoc. Not only has the United States failed to develop a coherent policy toward the conflict in Bosnia, but it has ignored the problems inherent in democratic transitions in ethnically divided countries. It has encouraged deeply divided societies to hold elections even in the absence of any provision to manage ethnic conflict. The success of the elections in Burundi was celebrated in Washington only weeks before the country was engulfed by a wave of brutal ethnic killings following an attempted coup d'état by the predominantly Tutsi army that feared the new elected Hutu-dominated government.

The challenges presented by the increase in ethnic conflict are complex, and it is not surprising that neither the parties to the conflict nor the international community have been able to formulate adequate responses. But nationalism is not a temporary phenomenon that will disappear naturally in a few years. Present conflicts are likely to last a long time and new ones will appear. This suggests the need for clear policy regarding nationalism—particularly in its early stages, before problems escalate out of control as happened in Yugoslavia.

The United States has responded so far to the individual crises created by nationalism without formulating an overall policy. Again, this is not surprising. It is also dangerous, because there is a demonstration effect that cannot be overemphasized at present. Each country and movement watch closely how the international community deals with these cases, seeking ways of legitimizing their own demands and of convincing the rest of the world that they deserve acceptance. Homeland leaders resisting reincorporation in South Africa drew encouragement from the break-up of the Soviet Union. The handling of minorities in one part of the world can become the example followed elsewhere. The division of Bosnia into ethnic enclaves may be unavoidable at present. But by sponsoring the Vance-Owen plan and successive versions of the partition, the international community also sends a message that nationalists everywhere will interpret as an acknowledgment that multi-ethnic states cannot function. How can the international community press Xhosas, Zulus, and Afrikaners to live peacefully in one state, when it recognizes that Serbs, Croats, and Bosnian Muslims can at best coexist when protected by a complex edifice of federations and confederations?

The response of the international community is probably most important after a secession, to prevent the onset of the vicious circle that creates ever more nationalist outbreaks. This cycle is predictable: new countries come into existence as an act of self-determination by one ethnic group; this majority group is very threatening to the minorities; these minorities respond with their own nationalism. Two cases of this second wave of conflict, in Croatia and Slovakia, will be discussed in this essay.

The European cases suggest that a crucial factor in preventing the onset of the vicious circle is the treatment of minorities: how they are dealt with by the countries in which they reside, how they relate to neighboring countries where that ethnic group constitutes the majority, and what their own demands are. How these problems are handled may determine whether a political opening leads toward democratization or toward domestic and international conflict.

Three of the four countries discussed here have divided in the period under discussion—only South Africa remains territorially intact. This creates some confusion concerning names. The problem is relatively simple concerning Czechoslovakia, because both the country and the name disappeared in January 1993, replaced by Slovakia and the Czech Republic. In the case of Ethiopia, too, the problem is relatively simple. While Eritrea remained part of Ethiopia until May 1993, the two were de facto separate entities for most of the period under consideration, and the names will be used to reflect this division. The major problem concerns Yugoslavia, since even after the break-up of the old country a new state by that name, comprising Serbia and Montenegro, remains in existence. To avoid confusion, the name Yugoslavia is used only to refer to the old Yugoslavia. The new Yugoslavia is referred to as Serbia, reflecting the political reality.

Part II.
Political Openings and Ethnic Conflict

INTRODUCTION

■ CZECHOSLOVAKIA, YUGOSLAVIA, ETHIOPIA, AND SOUTH AFRICA may not appear at first to have much in common. Indeed, Czechs and Yugoslavs with whom the author discussed this project have been extraordinarily reluctant to entertain the idea that their countries might share common problems with Africa. However, nationalist organizations in Ethiopia and even more clearly in South Africa have been observing developments in Eastern Europe with a great deal of interest, in the hope of finding in those examples arguments to strengthen their cause in the eyes of the world.

Upon closer analysis, the parallels are striking. In Czechoslovakia, Yugoslavia, and Ethiopia the process of political opening was derailed by mounting nationalist conflict, leading to partition and to the reappearance of nationalism in some of the new states. In South Africa, farther behind on the road of transition from the old political system, ethnic nationalism came close to disrupting the first universal suffrage elections in April 1994. The elections were saved at the eleventh hour by concessions made to Zulu nationalists, but these measures created new problems.

Thus, in all four cases, disturbing questions arise: Did the political opening cause the outbreak of nationalism, halting the process of democratization? And what are the implications of this link between political opening and ethnic nationalism for the U.S. policy of encouraging democratization in all countries?

YUGOSLAVIA

■ YUGOSLAVIA IS A DRAMATIC EXAMPLE of a country where the first multi-party elections since World War II were quickly followed by disintegration. Nevertheless, it would be wrong to conclude that democratization triggered a wave of ethnic nationalism. The problem started much earlier, and indeed it prevented any real movement toward democracy. The elections held in all the republics starting in April 1990 were intended to pave the way for the transformation of those republics into fully independent nation-states rather than to lay the foundation of a democratic system.[2]

That the secession of the new states should have been preceded by multi-party, supposedly democratic, elections had more to do with the climate of the time in Eastern Europe than with the presence of a real democratizing impulse. In Yugoslavia as elsewhere, multi-party elections were seen as the means to put an end to the communist government. The old regime was resented during the 1980s because of its ideological orientation and, most important, because it did not satisfy the demands of any population group or region. It was too decentralized to satisfy the Serbs, who are dispersed over a large part of the country and thus favor a more centralized structure. It was not decentralized enough to satisfy some of the minority groups, like the Albanians, who did not have their own republic, but only the autonomous region of Kosovo within the Serbian republic. In turn, the autonomy of Kosovo was a thorn in the side of the Serbs, who considered the region the cradle of their civilization and wanted it to be fully part of Serbia. In addition, richer, more industrialized republics such as Slovenia resented the fact that they were subsidizing the least developed areas of the country.

Relations between the federal center and the republics were not the only cause of discontent. Yugoslavia had experienced serious economic problems for a decade. Nevertheless, nationalist rather than economic demands drove the process of change. Indeed, the belated attempt by the federal government under Prime Minister Ante Marković to start a process of economic restructuring in 1989 was lost in the upsurge of nationalism which by that time dominated Yugoslav politics.

Several factors explain the strength of nationalism and the weakness of the democratic drive in Yugoslavia. The multi-ethnic and multi-religious character of the country were of course important, but they do not provide a sufficient explanation. Multi-ethnic countries can survive and be democratic as well. In the case of Yugoslavia, however, the problems created by lack of homogeneity were compounded by the legacy of the open and brutal conflicts during World War II, when both Serbian and Croatian militias indulged in violence based not only on ideological differences, but also on ethnic hatred. After the war, all groups managed to live fairly peacefully in one country for over 40 years. Nevertheless, there remained a large reservoir of bitter memories that were easily evoked by nationalist leaders and organizations.

A more important reason for the prevalence of nationalist impulses over democratic ones was that in the late 1960s and 1970s Tito (Josip Broz) deliberately played nationalism against demands for liberalization, even while seeking to contain nationalism within limits compatible with the rule of the communist party. Committed to Yugoslavism, in the immediate postwar period the communist leadership sought to downplay ethnic differences. By the 1960s the government faced a multitude of pressures and demands: for more economic reform in the direction of market socialism; for the strengthening of the participatory, democratic component of the system of self-management; for greater geographic decentralization and enhanced power for the republics; and more broadly for greater political space for different groups.

Unable to ignore or repress all demands, Tito in the end settled for accepting nationalist aspirations, instead of increased pluralism or more extensive economic change. In the early 1970s, a regime crackdown on reformers was accompanied by a change of the federal structure that strengthened the power of the republics and gave the autonomous regions of Vojvodina and Kosovo, nominally part of Serbia, a status almost on par with that of the six republics. By the late 1970s, the League of Yugoslav Communists, the glue that kept Yugoslavia together, had also been decentralized into eight separate but equally authoritarian machines. In other words, the regime made concessions to nationalist aspirations to blunt demands for the reform of the communist system, but it then frustrated nationalist aspirations by keeping all republics under the control of party machines sharing the same ideology and goals.

The transfer of power from the federal government to the republics did not make the system more pluralistic, because the communist party continued to rule. Nor did it solve the problem of ethnic relations, since the new republics, far from having homogeneous populations, contained large minorities. The Serbs, a large percentage of whom live outside Serbia, were particularly unhappy about the reforms. Their desire to be united within one state was best satisfied by a unitary Yugoslavia, or at least one in which the republics had limited autonomy. Furthermore,

Serbia resented the autonomous status given to the Vojvodina and particularly to Kosovo, where, they felt, the Serbs had become an endangered minority.

It has been argued that in an attempt to fashion a viable structure for a multi-ethnic state, the Soviet Union had allowed the republics to take on the "characteristics of independent states that have lost their independence."[3] To some extent, this was true in Yugoslavia as well. Such systems can easily disintegrate. As long as the communist party remained solidly in control, the problem was minimized. Any weakening of the party, however, threatened the unity of the country.

Tito's death in 1980 marked the beginning of the process that eventually led to the break-up of the country. The passing of the old guard, who believed in Yugoslavism and had adopted a more decentralized system only as a matter of political expediency, also coincided with an economic turning point. After growing steadily from the end of World War II, per capita income started decreasing sharply after 1980, so that by the end of the decade it had plummeted to the level of the late 1960s.[4] With the death of Tito, the communist leadership lost the legitimacy gained through the wartime victory, but it could not forge a new legitimacy based on its more recent accomplishments.

The response to the deteriorating situation took two different forms. At the center, a cadre of technocrats sought to develop a reform strategy to deal with the critical economic problems. In the republics, the mounting dissatisfaction found expression in increasingly militant nationalism. The federal government was slow to adopt economic or political reform. Significant change was introduced only with the constitutional amendments of November 1988 and the economic reforms undertaken after March 1989 by Prime Minister Ante Marković. The reforms aimed at liberalizing the economy, reducing state interference, strengthening market mechanisms, and facilitating foreign investment. Economic measures, particularly painful structural adjustment, are not a popular cause, nor do they bring about quick results. They were not an antidote to increasingly militant nationalism.

As in most countries, ethnic nationalism had conflicting expressions in Yugoslavia. Serbian nationalism aimed at keeping Yugoslavia together, strengthening the federal government, and limiting the autonomy of the republics and regions. The Greater Serbia embracing all territories where Serbs lived was Yugoslavia itself. But Slovenian and Croatian nationalism was a drive to break away from the federation, which was seen as a vehicle for Serbian control. Thus nationalism was simultaneously a centralizing and a disintegrating force.

Neither response to the crisis—economic reform or nationalism—favored democracy. Economic reform was the domain of technocrats, not a matter for popular participation and open discussion. Nationalism was embraced, and in Serbia orchestrated, by the communist elites. They agitated for the right of their particular group to self-determination but were oblivious to the rights of other ethnic groups. By focusing exclusively on the group, the nationalists further reduced the space for individual choices—the precondition for democracy. Being a nationalist in Serbia or Croatia in the late 1980s was not an option, it was a duty.

Democratic reform, mostly limited to a call for multi-party elections, came late and suddenly. It also started at the level of the republics, with the multi-party elections in Slovenia and Croatia in April 1990, followed by elections in other republics by the end of the year. Federal multi-party elections, on the other hand, never took place. In July 1990 Prime Minister Marković tried to launch a Yugoslav-wide party, the Alliance of Reform Forces, to run against nationalist parties in federal elections, but it was too late. Slovenia and Croatia had already gone to the polls, and the remaining republics were about to do the same. The republics' leadership was no longer interested in the federal government.

The holding of republic-level elections before national ones may have sealed the disintegration of Yugoslavia. Juan Linz and Alfred Stepan argue that among countries that held democratic "founding elections" in the presence of strong nationalist movements, those that survived intact held national elections before regional ballots, forcing the parties, as well as the electorate, to focus on common problems, rather than on the special interests of the individual regions.[5] On the other hand, in countries that held local and regional elections first, the parties and the electorate were encouraged to focus on particularistic issues, so that a common arena was never developed. While such conclusions may confuse to some extent cause and effect—in countries that held regional elections first nationalism may have been stronger to begin with—a reform process starting at the regional level undeniably accentuated divisions instead of areas of commonality.

By mid-1990, Yugoslavia was well on its way to breaking up. Political activity was concentrated in the republics, whose leaders all came from the old communist apparatus but had given themselves a new identity and had been elected in a new process. The largely unreformed federal government still represented the old system. Slovenia and Croatia proclaimed their independence. They promptly received diplomatic recognition from Germany, but it is doubtful that even withholding such recognition would have made much difference at that point. (An earlier, concerted attempt by the international community to help Yugoslavia reform its federal system could conceivably have prevented the break-up, but on this point one can only speculate.)

Secession did not bring about peace: the same ethnic nationalism that caused the republics to seek independence also led to civil war. A militant Croatian government was a threat to the Serbian minority within its borders, while a militant Serbia was a threat to all the other republics and to the non-Serbian populations of Kosovo and Vojvodina. Militant nationalism, in other words, made it impossible not only to keep the federation together, but also to keep the republics together. Croatia, Serbia, and Bosnia-Herzegovina were soon deep into conflict, while Kosovo and Macedonia were cauldrons ready to explode. Only Slovenia, blessed with a homogeneous population and sharing no border with Serbia, escaped the crisis.

Ethnic nationalism in Yugoslavia was not caused by democratization. Nationalism had remained a strong force under socialism, but the communist leadership had succeeded in controlling and even using it. The death of Tito and the passing of the old guard started weakening the communist hold that had served as an antidote to nationalism. Serbian militancy increased through the decade. However, the final blow to Yugoslavia was the political opening of 1989–1990. A political opening provides greater opportunities for all forces, not just new democratic ones. The already significant nationalist forces quickly took advantage of the new opportunities.

In turn, nationalism reduced the chances that the opening would lead toward democratization. Bogged down in internal conflict and war against each other, the new republics moved farther than ever from a democratic transformation.

ETHIOPIA

■ THERE ARE PARALLELS between Ethiopia and Yugoslavia, but also important differences. In both countries, nationalism was already strong before a political opening took place, and the drive toward democratization can at best be defined as extremely weak. In Ethiopia after 1991, a definite, and so far relatively successful, attempt was also made by the central government to manipulate ethnic nationalism to divide and rule, encouraging, and indeed forcing, the ethnicization of politics. In a way reminiscent of what happened in Yugoslavia in the 1970s, the Ethiopian government used ethnic nationalism as an antidote to liberalization.

Ethnic nationalism in Ethiopia became an important phenomenon after the overthrow of Emperor Haile Selassie in a military coup in 1974. Resentment against the imperial power, particularly strong in those areas of the country conquered at the turn of the century, certainly existed earlier, but it was not articulated in a doctrine of the right of ethnic groups to self-determination. Eritrean nationalism, which originated in the 1950s when a United Nations' decision made the former Italian colony part of Ethiopia, was not ethnic-based, either. Eritrean nationalists accepted the multi-ethnic country defined by the colonial borders and sought independence for it. In fact, after Eritrea became independent in 1993, its president made clear that political parties and movements articulating ethnic demands and drawing their support from only one ethnic group would not be tolerated. Like the African leaders of the 1960s, President Isaias Afewerki sought to use the state to create a nation.

The revolution of 1974, which eventually brought the self-proclaimed Marxist-Leninist regime of Mengistu Haile Mariam to power, briefly opened political space in the country. It was filled first by organizations of the civilian left, seeking their own brand of Marxist-Leninist regime under civilian leadership. When those organizations were destroyed by the military government during the Red Terror period of 1977–78, the banner of resistance was picked up by the ethnic liberation movements.

The two most important were the Tigrean People's Liberation Front (TPLF) in the north and the Oromo Liberation Front (OLF) in the south. The TPLF, which drew its support from the small Tigrean population, was centralized and cohesive, and strongly supported by the Eritrean nationalists. The movement declared itself not only Marxist-Leninist, but also "pro-Albanian," a code word used in the 1980s by organizations rejecting the reform process under way in China and the Soviet Union, and idealizing Albania as the model of pure socialism. The OLF, potentially the most important movement since the Oromos represent about 40 percent of Ethiopia's population, never succeeded in developing either a clear ideology or a cohesive structure. Weak and divided leadership and poor organization compounded the underlying problem of the absence of a state tradition and of a strong common identity among the geographically dispersed and culturally diverse Oromo groups.

The Mengistu regime reacted to ethnic nationalism primarily as it did to all opposition, by trying to crush it with the force of arms. But it belatedly also attempted to provide a political framework that would accommodate nationalism without decreasing central control. Superficially, the framework was the one employed by the Soviet Union with apparent success for decades: dividing the country into ethnic regions with a degree of self-government and granting special autonomous status to particular areas, all under the iron hand of a strong, centralized party. But the reform came very late, the amount of power transferred to the regions was minor, and the nationalist movements were strong, particularly in Eritrea and Tigrai. As a result, the maneuver was unsuccessful.

In May 1991, the TPLF, with the support of the Eritrean nationalists, brought down the Mengistu regime and entered Addis Ababa. In the final period, the rebels acquired the support of the United States which, anxious to avoid the bloodbath of a battle for the Ethiopian capital, helped negotiate the surrender of the care-taker regime installed after Mengistu fled the country.

The victorious TPLF faced two dilemmas. The most important was that of holding the country together. That Eritrea would get its independence was a foregone conclusion, but the front aspired to control the rest of Ethiopia, not merely a tiny, independent Tigrai. The TPLF was also an ethnic liberation movement, however, representing about 12 percent of the population residing in a very impoverished region. It was thus poorly placed to control a country already rent asunder by conflicting nationalisms. The second dilemma faced by TPLF leader Meles Zenawi, the former pro-Albanian communist, was how to satisfy the U.S. demands for democratic reform, thus maintaining the support of the United States. The TPLF quickly shed its Marxist-Leninist ideological baggage, at least outwardly. A more complex undertaking was holding elections while safeguarding control.

The decision was made to rely on TPLF-controlled ethnic organizations to oppose the autonomous nationalist groups, while going through the motions of multi-party elections. Some of these TPLF-controlled ethnic organizations had been set-up in the last period of the war against Mengistu, when the TPLF extended its operations outside the boundaries of Tigrai and needed to change its image as a purely Tigrean movement. Others came into existence quickly in 1991. All these groups operated under the umbrella of the Ethiopian People's Democratic Revolutionary Front (EPRDF). It was officially the EPRDF that entered Addis Ababa in May 1991, but the TPLF controlled the organization.

An all-party conference held in Addis Ababa in July 1991 created a transitional government, consisting of a national council and a cabinet including representatives from both TPLF-aligned and independent ethnic organizations, but dominated by the EPRDF. It also agreed to a two-and-a-half year transition process, starting with elections for regional and local councils and continuing with the election of a constituent assembly, the approval of a constitution, and finally the election of a national assembly and government.

In preparation for the elections, the government divided the country into 14 new regions, gerrymandered to be as ethnically homogeneous as possible. While most regions remained in reality very diverse, each was identified as being the domain of one ethnic group—or in some cases of several.

The local and regional elections of June 1992 strengthened the ethnic division of the country. No real national parties, only ethnic ones, competed for power in specific regions or subregions. This ensured the fragmentation of the opposition, while the existence of the EPRDF brought all pro-TPLF parties together. Not content with this advantage, the EPRDF also did its best to keep the autonomous parties from registering their candidates. This caused the withdrawal from the elections, and shortly thereafter from the government, of the most important of these parties, and caused the OLF to go to war against the EPRDF.[6] The elections were thus a set-back for democratization: they turned into a de facto single-party exercise, destroyed the tenuous broad-based alliance in the July 1991 government of national unity, and increased resentment against the EPRDF in many parts of the country.

Neither did the elections help to reduce ethnic conflict. Most visibly and dramatically, they led instead to a resurgence of fighting between the TPLF and the OLF, which only subsided several months later, after the TPLF succeeded in capturing thousands of OLF fighters and supporters. The more long lasting impact of these severely flawed elections was that they forced all political debate to focus on ethnic issues. Ethiopia had to devise policies to address its enormous social and economic problems, the consequence of underdevelopment and drought compounded by bad economic policies and war. No party raised these issues, which affected all Ethiopians. Instead, the elections were dominated by ethnic relations, particularly what the opposition considered to be the TPLF's attempt to impose its rule. The deliberate ethnicization of Ethiopian politics thus led to the narrowing of political discourse.

As in the case of Yugoslavia, the increased ethnic tensions were not the result of a process of democratization. The Meles regime was less repressive than its predecessor, but not conspicuously democratic. The drive toward democracy came from the outside, from the aid donors, and above all from the United States. The result was a respect for the form of democracy—elections were held—but without the content, the element of voter's choice without which there is no democracy. In this game between democratic form and content, ethnicity became an instrument deliberately used by the government to limit choice.

. . . .

CZECHOSLOVAKIA

■   OF THE FOUR CASES PRESENTED HERE, Czechoslovakia provides the strongest evidence of a causal link between a political opening and the emergence of ethnic nationalisms strong enough to destroy the country. Beginning in November 1989, Czechoslovakia experienced a groundswell of popular support for liberalization and democratization. A wave of massive popular demonstrations spread from Prague to other cities, and they were undeniably pro-democracy, not nationalist. Within three years, however, nationalist Slovak politicians caused the country to split into a Czech and a Slovak republic, despite indications that the majority of the population, even in Slovakia, wanted a looser union, not complete separation.

Without much conflict, Czechoslovakia slipped into partition, a development strongly influenced by the division of Yugoslavia and the Soviet Union into their ethnic components. The Czech Republic continued the process of democratization and economic liberalization. In Slovakia, however, former communists returned to power under the new nationalist facade, and political and economic reform virtually ground to a halt. Despite the lack of enthusiasm for partition among the general population, Slovak nationalism was strong and it did more than halt democratization. It also provoked the opposing nationalism of the large Hungarian minority, which felt threatened and thus mobilized in defense of what it saw as its rights. This raised the possibility of a vicious circle of ethnic conflict such as the one that led to civil war in Yugoslavia.

A typical Eastern European country with an ethnically diverse population and a history complicated enough to provide support for any number of conflicting nationalist claims, Czechoslovakia has suffered chronic but not acute ethnic tensions in the post-World War II period. Czechoslovakia was a new country, established with the Versailles Treaty after World War I, bringing together pieces of the former Austro-Hungarian empire with diverse history. The population was a mix of Czech, Slovak, German, Hungarian, Roma (Gypsy), and Ruthenian groups. Making matters more complicated, before the break-up of the Austro-Hungarian empire, the eastern part of the country, with its Slovak, Hungarian, and Ruthenian population, had been ruled from Hungary; the western part, from Austria. The new Czech republic was short-lived. It started being partitioned along ethnic lines in 1938 when Hitler forced it to cede to Germany, Hungary, and Poland the territories inhabited by the respective population groups. The process was completed in 1939, when Slovakia seceded, and what was left of Czechoslovakia was turned into a protectorate of the Third Reich. Both the secession of Slovakia and the annexation by Hungary of the territory inhabited by Hungarians created precedents that came back to haunt Czechoslovakia after 1989.

Czechoslovakia was reconstituted after World War II. As in Yugoslavia, the socialist regime originally tried to ignore ethnic differences, creating a centralized system and stressing a new common socialist identity. As in Yugoslavia, the government eventually accepted nationalism as the lesser evil that could be used to combat the greater threat of liberalization. In 1968, the reformist movement known as the Prague Spring briefly threatened the communists' hold on power. The reforms introduced during the Prague Spring included the adoption of a federal system of government that recognized Slovakia as a separate entity with its own national assembly—the Slovak National Council—and government. In other words, the political opening of 1968 was accompanied by the manifestation of Slovak nationalist aspirations and their recognition by the Czechs. The repression of the Prague Spring by the Soviets led to the abrogation of all reforms, except for the new federal structure. As in Yugoslavia, the government appeared to consider nationalism a lesser threat and a useful safety valve to defuse the greater danger of liberalization.

In the following years, the government attempted to develop the Slovak economy and to close the gap between Slovakia and the western part of the country. Nevertheless, the area remained depressed. There was little manifest opposition to the communist regime anywhere in Czechoslovakia in this period. In Prague, opposition was limited to a small group of dissident intellectuals—Vàclav Havel was the best known—determined to maintain their intellectual honesty although they had few illusions about changing the government. In Bratislava, resentment with the status quo found expression in what an observer defined as "a lurking Slovak nationalism."[7]

The demonstrations that began in late 1989 originated in Prague among students, but as the movement spread the old dissidents immediately took over the leadership. Within days, a broad-based organization came into existence, the Civic Forum. It became immediately clear that in this uprising Slovaks would go their own way. An organization similar to the Civic Forum, called Public Against Violence, was formed in Slovakia. There was neither hostility between the two organizations nor difference of goals. Simply, one was Czech and the other Slovak.

The Czech lands and Slovakia continued to drift apart, although in the 1990 elections nationalist parties received limited support even in Slovakia. As the leaders began to tackle the concrete problems of the transition from socialism—from economic reform to the writing of a new constitution—Slovak representatives articulated a different agenda, putting nationalist concerns ahead of everything else and rejecting discussion of economic reform as an anti-Slovak policy. With an economic base concentrated in heavy industry, mining, and weapon manufacturing, Slovakia was bound to suffer the most in the short run from economic reform that aimed at removing government subsidies to inefficient concerns. It was also bound to find privatization most difficult. The Slovaks' fears that they would be the losers in the reform process were worsened by the new government's announcement that Czechoslovakia should stop exporting weapons (a policy since reversed), a decision likely to increase unemployment in the already depressed Slovak area.

The slide into partition was unexpectedly swift. During 1991, President Vàclav Havel, musing on the problems facing Czechoslovakia, acknowledged the strength of Slovak nationalism, and even professed understanding for it, but also argued that splitting Czechoslovakia could be avoided.[8] A year later, after endless discussions on a new constitution and a new form of federalism, Czech and Slovak leaders decided to divide the country, without benefit of a referendum. Opinion polls showed a public divided about partition. In a summer 1992 survey, for example, 46 percent of respondents favored partition and 45 percent opposed it in the Czech lands, while 41 percent favored the split and 46 percent opposed it in Slovakia. Yet over 80 percent of respondents in both republics saw partition as inevitable.[9] Even after the break-up, Slovaks remained unenthusiastic about the separation, with 51 percent of respondents believing the split represented a loss, and only 32 percent declaring that they welcomed the separation.[10]

The political opening of 1989 provided the political space that allowed the manifestation and growth of Slovak nationalism, leading to the independence of Slovakia. It was a remarkably peaceful process, because it was not opposed by the Czech authorities. Democratization thus did lead to the break-up of Czechoslovakia—but the break-up did not have to be an obstacle to further democratization. Indeed it was not in the Czech Republic.

This peaceful transformation, however, is not the entire story of the relations between democratization and nationalism in the former Czechoslovakia. Militant Slovak nationalism, in turn, stirred the nationalism of the Hungarian minority, reviving both fears of repression or forced assimilation and a nostalgia for the short-lived union with Hungary during World War II. The looming conflict became a threat to the consolidation of democracy and to peace in Slovakia.

Czechoslovakia thus illustrates four processes: the growth of ethnic nationalism in the political space provided by a democratic political opening; the manipulation of ethnic nationalism by politicians; the negative impact of ethnic nationalism on democratization; and the vicious circle that sets in when the nationalism of one group engenders the counterpoising nationalism of another.

. . . .

SOUTH AFRICA

■ DEMOCRACY AND ETHNIC NATIONALISM have a long and complex history in South Africa. Each needs to be surveyed separately before the relationship between them can be addressed.

None of the political organizations competing for power in South Africa during the apartheid years put democracy high on its agenda, and certainly not western-style democracy. Typical of other liberation movements on the continent, the African National Congress (ANC) demanded the transfer of power from the white minority to the majority and advocated government control of the country's major economic assets. Until 1990, the ANC appeared more inclined toward a single-party system and a statist economy than toward western-style democracy and a free market system.

Paradoxically, the National Party (NP) was also a liberation movement—an Afrikaner liberation movement—that had succeeded in coming to power in 1948 and had stayed there ever since. While formally competing with other parties in whites-only elections, during 40 years in power the NP had created a system that had more in common with single-party than with democratic ones. There was no real distinction between state and party. The NP penetrated all institutions—the bureaucracy and the military in the first place. Like all African single-parties, the NP also used its control over the large parastatal sector of the economy to dispense patronage, maintain support, and advance the cause of the ethnic group it represented.

The third organization to play an important role after 1990 was Inkatha. Officially a cultural movement during the apartheid years, Inkatha was in reality the single party of the KwaZulu homeland, controlled in a very autocratic fashion by KwaZulu Chief Minister Mangosuthu Buthelezi. After the unbanning of the ANC, Inkatha tried briefly to recast itself as a moderate, democratic, multi-ethnic political party, only to return openly to a platform of Zulu nationalism.

South Africa thus moved into the final stage of the transition from apartheid to majority rule with a political arena dominated by three organizations with nondemocratic traditions. The issue of democracy was nevertheless at the center of the political agenda, not because the participants believed in it, but because of the reality that no group could eliminate the others. Furthermore, by 1990 no organization aspiring to international respectability could afford not to speak the language of democracy.

The ANC's initial concept of the transition was formally the most democratic—it advocated the election of a constituent assembly by universal suffrage and the transfer of power to a government elected under the new constitution. Other organizations, however, feared that the outcome of such process would be all but democratic, because the ANC might get enough votes to dominate the constituent assembly, and later the government and parliament, creating a new de facto single-party system. The NP thus dismissed majority rule as undemocratic, seeking first some form of group representation, and then a power-sharing formula that would decrease the weight of the ANC and increase that of other parties, particularly its own. Inkatha, the weakest of the three organizations, first cast around in the direction of an alliance with the NP. Eventually, it settled for a platform of Zulu nationalism, seeking a system that would maximize the power of regions, thus allowing Buthelezi to maintain his control over KwaZulu.

Nevertheless, a genuine political opening took place in South Africa after 1990, and an element of democracy was introduced in the transition process by the existence of countervailing forces. In a country where even quoting ANC leaders had been prohibited, political debate became suddenly quite open and the press much freer. Independent organizations multiplied, a process that had started in the 1980s, but under much more difficult conditions and with continuous government interference. Finally, the NP and the ANC came to admit that the transition would not take place along the lines they had envisaged and that they would have to compromise much more than they had been planning to do. They also accepted that other groups, including those they loathed, should be included in the negotiations. The NP swallowed the presence of the South African Communist Party, while the ANC accepted the presence of the despised leaders of the homelands. Over 20 organizations were eventually invited to the negotiating table.

The process was far from smooth, and democratization was not willingly and enthusiastically accepted by all parties. Some refused to join the negotiations; others joined but quit. Most opponents of the agreement emerging between the ANC and the NP rallied by 1993 around the banner of ethnic nationalism. The standard bearers of ethnic nationalism became the Inkatha Freedom Party; the Afrikaner organizations refusing to accept the transition envisaged by President F. W. de Klerk, which came together in the Afrikaner Volkfront under the leadership of retired General Constand Viljoen; and the leaders of two of the "independent homelands," Bophuthatswana and the Ciskei. Together, they formed the Concerned South Africans Group (COSAG), later renamed the Freedom Alliance.

It was purely an alliance of convenience. The organizations were united only by their opposition to a unitary South Africa or to a federal one where the states would be territories without an ethnic identity. Buthelezi wanted a Zulu state; nationalist Afrikaners, their own homeland. Inevitably, the alliance failed to maintain its cohesion. The leaders of Bophuthatswana and the Ciskei did not succeed in evoking a nationalist response in their respective homelands. As elections approached in April 1994, only Buthelezi and the most extremist Afrikaner organizations openly refused to participate in the process, and even Buthelezi joined at the last minute. Among Afrikaners and Zulus, the embers of ethnic nationalism remain, suggesting that the problem will flare up again in the future.

The emergence of ethnic nationalism as a central problem in South Africa on the eve of the transition from apartheid and in the wake of a major political opening is somewhat more difficult to explain than in Yugoslavia, Czechoslovakia, or even Ethiopia. In those countries, ethnic nationalism had been a force barely kept in check by authoritarian regimes. In South Africa, the vast majority of the black population had resisted the separate ethnic identities that the apartheid regime tried to impose, yet nationalism began manifesting itself precisely as apartheid was being dismantled.

The "grand apartheid" design was to transform South Africa from a unitary country where whites were a minority into a constellation of nominally independent ethnic states. The white state, with 87 percent of the land and almost all economic assets, would dominate, thus perpetuating white rule under a different guise. To succeed, the plan required blacks to identify with their respective homelands. The development of strong ethnic identities was, however, so clearly a tool of the white government that it was resisted. Far from happily accepting political rights within separate independent homelands, South Africa's diverse, disenfranchised population continued to fight for the common goal of political rights in a united South Africa. Narrow ethnic identification among blacks was weakened by the overriding importance of the common oppression they experienced because of their race.

With the transition from apartheid, however, ethnicity became a tool that black leaders, too, could use to shape the new South Africa so as to suit their needs. The long-awaited transition was dangerous for whites but also for the homeland establishment—that is, for blacks who had cooperated with the apartheid regime and had been granted positions of power in the homeland structures, or even for the homeland civil servants, who might lose their jobs after reintegration of the homelands in South Africa. Ethnic nationalism became the tool of homeland leaders unwilling to give up their positions of power and return to obscurity.

Three homeland leaders, Chief Buthelezi in KwaZulu, Lucas Mangope in Bophuthatswana, and Oupa Gqoso in the Ciskei in particular decided to play the nationalist card. This required them to recast the image of the homelands from creations of the apartheid system, ludicrously made up of scattered fragments of barren land, to genuine nation-states deprived of their independence and much of their historical territory by the white regime. To strengthen their case, the leaders deliberately drew parallels between their situation and that of new countries emerging in Europe and Central Asia after the break-down of the socialist system. If the Baltic states had a right to self-determination, so did the Zulu and Tswana nations. History, traditions, and national celebrations were quickly rediscovered or invented to complete the picture of the nation-state. Mangope even went as far as inviting delegations from Lithuania, Ukraine, and Khazikstan for an official visit to Bophuthatswana.

Lucas Mangope and Oupa Gqoso failed to gain credibility with their own groups, and in early 1994 they were forced to give up their fight against reintegration of their homelands into South Africa. Buthelezi was more successful. The existence of the nineteenth century Zulu empire provided Zulu nationalism with some historical foundation, although the empire had comprised only a small part of modern-day KwaZulu. The size of the Zulu population, over seven million, also added some substance to the concept of a Zulu nation. Buthelezi himself had a long, if ambiguous, history of opposition to apartheid and a strong political organization in KwaZulu. He thus succeeded in gaining a following, but at the cost of dividing the Zulus among themselves. Bloody battles between Inkatha and ANC supporters had first broken out in KwaZulu in the 1980s and continued through the transition period, extending to the area around Johannesburg, where nationalism found a particularly responsive chord among the Zulu migrant workers living in the hostels.

Organizations embracing ethnic nationalism were not the only threat to democratization in South Africa. During the election campaign, followers of every political party showed intolerance and engaged in intimidation and violence. Some of the worst violence arose from the fighting between nationalist and non-nationalist Zulus. Even this fighting, however, hinged on whether or not ethnic groups should be recognized in the political organization of the new South Africa.

Ethnic nationalism is bound to remain important in the coming years. It will offer an easy rallying point for the discontent that will inevitably follow the transition, when it becomes apparent that not even the new government can do much to address immediately the enormous backlog of economic and social problems. Nevertheless, in 1994, ethnic nationalism in South Africa is still far from the force it is today in Yugoslavia, Czechoslovakia, or Ethiopia, countries either already disintegrated or in real danger of disintegrating. South Africa still has the opportunity to manage the tensions and continue the transition to a democratic form of government rather than simply control by the black majority. Nevertheless, all the ingredients for a major problem are there: leaders determined to play the ethnic card to further their political ambitions; economic and social problems no government can solve in the short run; a political opening that creates space for all organizations, not just democratic ones; and the prospect of a redistribution of political and economic power that increases competition. Such conditions are a breeding ground for any kind of undemocratic movements. In the post-Cold War era, in an ethnically diverse country, these various pressures could very easily manifest themselves through heightened ethnic conflict, as has happened in many places around the world. Future institutions and policies will be all important to the outcome.

. . . .
CONCLUSIONS

■   DEMOCRATIZATION WAS NOT THE CAUSE of ethnic conflict in the countries discussed. In Ethiopia and Yugoslavia, open ethnic conflict preceded, and thwarted, the political opening. In Czechoslovakia, ethnic nationalism blossomed in the new political space, but it had strong historical precedents. In South Africa, ethnic conflict was facilitated by the removal of the common enemy.

No protracted liberalization and democratization process preceded the collapse of the old authoritarian regime in any of these countries. The old systems were brought down by war (Ethiopia), economic sanctions and prolonged civil unrest (South Africa), or by the general collapse of socialist regimes (Yugoslavia and Czechoslovakia). No matter what the proximate causes, all transitions provided opportunities for previously

OVERSEAS DEVELOPMENT COUNCIL

32

suppressed political forces. These limited openings, far short of democratization, allowed ethnically based parties to emerge, greatly increasing the intensity of ethnic tensions and the scope of ethnic demands. An opening provides opportunities for all political forces. In countries with a diverse population, nationalism is a force certain to manifest itself under such circumstances.

In a different time period, without the example of triumphant nationalism elsewhere, the problem might have been contained. This was probably not true in Yugoslavia, which had been moving toward crisis for a decade. In the other countries, the problem might not have arisen so strongly, particularly in Czechoslovakia, with its reluctant slide into partition, or in South Africa, with its history of resistance to forced ethnicization. Speculation does not help—the demonstration effect of ethnic nationalism today is overwhelming.

Part III.
The Vicious Circle

INTRODUCTION

■ THE EXPLOSION OF ETHNIC NATIONALISM that accompanied the initial opening in Yugoslavia, Czechoslovakia, South Africa, and Ethiopia was not an event of short duration, but the onset of a long-term problem. Where it occurred, secession has not proven to be a solution. Some of the successor states face the mobilization of their own ethnic minorities, fearful of being dominated and discriminated against. In all countries, democratization is threatened. Finding means of breaking the vicious circle by containing and managing nationalism is thus essential to further progress.

The original countries and their successor states attempted to break the vicious circle of ethnic conflict by writing constitutions, setting up institutions, and not least by political maneuvering. None of the countries successfully defused ethnic conflict. Their approaches varied widely, but a common issue recurred in all cases, namely, the impossibility of managing ethnic conflict without recognizing the rights of ethnic groups as groups, rather than simply the rights of their members as individuals. The problem of group rights thus emerged as a central theme in all cases.

The countries discussed in this chapter are by necessity not the original four, because three of them broke up under the impact of nationalist demands. Only South Africa remains intact. The number of successor states is too large to discuss them all—Yugoslavia broke into five new countries after 1990; Czechoslovakia, into two in January 1993; and Ethiopia into two in April 1993. One successor will be discussed for each country, namely the new Ethiopia (without Eritrea), Croatia, and Slovakia. Ethiopia was chosen over Eritrea, and Slovakia over the Czech Republic, because ethnic conflict is more explosive in each. Croatia was singled out among the successor states of Yugoslavia because it also faces serious ethnic problems, but at the same time has not sunk into complete chaos— a study of Bosnia would be one of warfare, not of attempts to manage the vicious circle of ethnic conflict.

CROATIA AND SLOVAKIA

■   CROATIA AND SLOVAKIA SHOW some striking similarities in their approach to ethnic pluralism and conflict. Products of the break-up of multi-ethnic states, both countries had strong national identities; each represented the embodiment of the aspirations of a specific ethnic group to a country of its own. However, neither country was ethnically homogeneous, containing instead sizeable minorities. The initial approach to the problem of these minorities in both Croatia and Slovakia was deeply influenced by the intellectual baggage of the Soviet approach to the problem of the nationalities, based on a distinction between "constituent nationalities" and ethnic minorities. The constituent nationality was the largest ethnic group, the one to which the country primarily belonged. Minorities were not simply the less numerous groups, but those whose position vis-à-vis the state differed from that of the constituent nationality.[11] This classification thus created distinct categories of citizens and was inherently discriminatory, raising the fears and encouraging the nationalism of the minorities.

In both cases, the problem of dealing with ethnic minorities was greatly complicated by the relations with neighboring states. The Serb minority of Croatia was openly backed by Serbia. The Hungarian minority of Slovakia did not receive similar open support from the outside, but the Hungarian government continued to profess a deep interest in the fate of all ethnic Hungarians within and outside its borders. The Slovak government feared that interest would turn into irredentism and territorial revendications.

While their approach was deeply influenced by the old Soviet thinking, the Slovak and Croatian governments were also open to a different set of pressures concerning ethnic relations, those from institutions such as the European Union, the Council of Europe, and the Council for Security and Cooperation in Europe (CSCE). Anxious to be seen as integral parts of Europe, Croatia and Slovakia could not completely dismiss the pressure to respect certain principles concerning democracy and human rights, including the right of minorities to protection against both discrimination and forced assimilation. (These principles will be discussed in the next section.) As a result, Croatia and Slovakia also added the language of minority rights to their constitutions. The result was an unworkable mixture of Soviet and democratic concepts.

In the initial period after these countries attained their independence, the intense nationalism of the Croatian and Slovak majorities prevailed, combined with the intellectual mind-set of the socialist period. As a result, each country was unambiguously identified with one specific constituent ethnic group—as used in the respective constitutions, the terms Slovak and Croatian denoted ethnicity, not citizenship.

"The republic of Croatia is hereby established as the national state of the Croatian nation and a state of members of other nations and minorities who are citizens: Serbs, Moslems, Slovenes, Czechs, Slovaks, Italians, Hungarians, Jews and others . . ." proclaimed the constitution adopted in December 1990. Although it then proceeded to guarantee the minorities "equality with citizens of Croatian nationality and the realization of ethnic rights. . ." the document was essentially discriminatory, because it drew a clear distinction between two categories of citizens.[12] In fact, the demand of members of the minority groups, particularly the Serbs, that the constitution recognize the equal status of all citizens was most emphatically rejected by the Croatian majority.[13]

The attitude of the Croats toward the Serb minority was, if not justifiable, at least understandable, because the constitution was adopted against the background of the civil war between the Croatian majority and the Serbian minority that had erupted in the summer of 1990, before Croatia declared its independence. The strife eventually culminated in the decision by extremist Croatian Serbs, backed by Serbia, to set up their own separate "republic" in the territory known as the Krajina. It also led to the unsuccessful intervention by the United Nations directed at maintaining peace in the area until a permanent political solution was worked out.

Against this background of civil war, a less discriminatory constitution by itself would not have brought about ethnic harmony in Croatia. Militant Croatian Serbs wanted separation, and they were backed by the Belgrade government as part of its design to reconstitute a Greater Serbia. However, an unbiased constitution could have given more moderate Serbs an incentive to accept their status as Croatian citizens and thus to resist the appeal of the extremists. As it was, the new state dominated by the Croats offered very little to the Serbian minority, which was granted at best second-class status.

The inadequacy of the constitution was denounced by the European Union, which pressed the Croatian government to deal more satisfactorily with the rights of national minorities as a condition for obtaining international recognition. A law on national minorities enacted by the Croatian parliament in December 1991 failed to satisfy the European Union. The following May the parliament approved the new Constitutional Law of Human Rights and Freedoms and the Rights of National and Ethnic Communities or Minorities in the Republic of Croatia.[14]

The Constitutional Law provided an elaborate framework for the protection of national minorities. Besides the vast array of individual rights guaranteed to all citizens, the law recognized the minorities' right to organize themselves for the pursuit of cultural activities. Most important, the law also recognized the need to create special status districts, with autonomous or self-governing status, in areas inhabited predominantly by national minorities. At first glance, the law appeared to provide very far-reaching protection to national minorities, with clauses that would prevent both discrimination against them and forced assimilation.

One aspect of the law needs to be highlighted, however, namely the apparent determination to keep different communities separate from each other. This was particularly evident in the realm of education: the law called for separate schools for different language groups. This was striking because the language of the Croatian majority and that of the Serbian minority are very similar, although the Serbs use the Cyrillic and the Croats the Latin alphabet. In fact, in the former Yugoslavia, the language was known as Serbo-Croatian. The law specified that minorities were entitled to set up, with government funds or their own, schools "which in their own language and alphabet based on separate programmes adequately present their history, culture, and science." In the special status districts controlled by national minorities, the Croatian population had the right to set up separate schools, using its own language and alphabet, and following its own curriculum. In other words, the solution to pluralism chosen by the Croatian government was the apartheid one:

not bilingualism, but the complete separation of different ethnic groups into "own affairs" schools. Yet, as in the apartheid system, the two communities were clearly not equal.

Slovakia also enacted a constitution based on the distinction between the constituent nationality and minorities. "We, the Slovak Nation" adopt this constitution, declared the preamble to the Constitution of the Slovak Republic, adding only in the fourth paragraph, "together with members of national minorities and ethnic groups living in the Slovak Republic."[15] The president of the Slovak parliament explained that the Slovaks enjoyed "sovereignty as well as sovereign rights," implying that the minorities did not.[16] As in Croatia, the discriminatory language was deliberate. An attempt by the Hungarian representatives to change "We, the Slovak Nation" to "We, the citizens of Slovakia" was rejected by the Slovak majority in the parliament, causing the Hungarians to walk out in protest.

The constitution, nevertheless, recognized that all people have equal rights: "Fundamental rights shall be guaranteed in the Slovak Republic regardless of sex, race, color, language, faith, political affiliation or conviction, national or social origin, nationality or ethnic origin . . ." (Art.12). The constitution also recognized the right of national minorities or ethnic groups "to promote their cultural heritage with other citizens of the same national minority or ethnic group . . ." and even to be educated in a minority language and to use a minority language in official communications, all within the limits established by law. However, "The exercise of rights by citizens of a national minority guaranteed by the Constitution may not threaten the sovereignty or territorial integrity of the Slovak Republic or discriminate against other citizens" (Article 34).

Commenting on the constitution, the CSCE concluded that "implemented in good faith, the Slovak constitution would be consistent with CSCE standards . . . ," but the CSCE worried about the climate of official intolerance toward minorities and also about the numerous articles of the constitution that stipulated that laws could impose limits on the exercise of those rights.[17] As in the case of Croatia, the very distinction between the Slovak nation and the national minorities that underlies the constitution conjured up the vision of a system based on a principle of "separate but equal."

The provisions of the constitution and the law on minorities were only part of the problem. In both Croatia and Slovakia, treatment of the national minorities did not comply with even the official standards. In Croatia, the fault could not be entirely attributed to the government. The Serb-inhabited districts that should have been granted special self-governing status according to the Constitutional Law were outside government control, part of the self-proclaimed republic of the Serbian Krajina. But the Serbs remaining in the part of Croatia under government control encountered serious discrimination. CSCE reports showed that after 1990 many police officers, public enterprise managers, and public officials belonging to the Serb minority were ousted from their jobs. At times entire enterprises were declared bankrupt and closed down, only to reopen shortly afterwards without their Serb employees.[18] The Croatian Helsinki Committee also denounced frequent violations of the rights of the Serbian minority, in particular their eviction from the apartments they occupied.[19] Serbian members of the Croatian parliament, for their part, complained about the difficulty many ethnic Serbs encountered in obtaining certificates of Croatian citizenship and about the loss of pensions, apartments, work permits, passports, and old age and social insurance experienced by Serbs who had not obtained a citizenship certificate.[20] They also pointed to the many instances of destruction of houses occupied by Serbs.

Relations between the government and the minorities remained troubled in Slovakia as well. The most sensitive issue concerned the Hungarian minority, estimated by the census to constitute about 11 percent of the population. Suspected by the government of favoring secession and annexation to Hungary, the Hungarians, in turn, considered themselves repressed and discriminated against. Although the constitution recognized language and cultural rights, the government prohibited the use of the old Hungarian village names, the posting of bilingual signs, and the recording of Hungarian first names in birth registers. For a while, it even tried to impose the use of the Slavic grammatical endings on Hungarian women's names.

Most alarming to the Hungarians was a plan devised by the Slovak government in 1993 to divide Slovakia into new administrative units. Running north to south, the new districts would have caused Hungarians, who reside in an east-west strip along the country's southern border, to be a minority everywhere.[21]

The reaction was not long in coming. Within a year of Slovakia's independence, the Hungarian minority was beginning to organize. Some 3,000 Hungarian local government officials and members of parliament convened in Komárno, on the Hungarian border, on January 8, 1994. They demanded: the recognition of the "communal status" of the Hungarian minority in the constitution, the equal rights of "the Hungarian community" and "the Slovak nation" in the formation of the state, and the strengthening of the system of local government within districts so designed as to keep the Hungarian population together, allowing a measure of self-government.[22] The participants in the meeting also demanded that the Slovak government adhere to the "European *Charta* of Local Government."[23]

The demands expressed by the Hungarian representatives at the Komárno meeting were moderate in tone and deliberately conforming with the positions taken by the Council of Europe and the CSCE. But they greatly alarmed the Slovak government, which inevitably interpreted them in light of its own experience. Independent Slovakia was the outcome of the grievances of the Slovak minority in Czechoslovakia. Its leaders had found it impossible to devise a formula that would accommodate their desire for autonomy within the structure of a united Czechoslovakia. The new government was thus inclined to believe that the Hungarian minority would also ultimately refuse to remain part of Slovakia. The Hungarians' demand for local self-government and language rights, no matter how cautiously worded, was seen by the Slovak authorities as the first step on the slippery road to the secession of the Hungarian-inhabited areas and their annexation by Hungary. The vicious circle of conflicting nationalism risked emerging in Slovakia as well.

. . . .

SOUTH AFRICA

■   IN CROATIA AND SLOVAKIA, RECOGNITION of the group rights of minorities, alongside the individuals rights of all citizens, has emerged as the key to a solution to ethnic conflict that does not preclude further democratization. In South Africa, too, nationalist Zulus and Afrikaners demanded recognition of group rights. For the Zulus, this also meant a political role for traditional authorities. During the negotiations, the National Party and the ANC had to make some concessions on these issues. Recognition of group rights, however, had connotations of apartheid in South Africa, though it was seen in the European countries as democratic because it gave more protection and a stronger political voice to minorities. As a result, the interim constitution enacted in December 1993 to guide the country through the transition period skirted the recognition of group rights with many ambiguities. A last minute agreement between the NP and Inkatha days before the April 1994 elections de facto resulted in the recognition of the group rights of the Zulus, with far reaching implications for all other groups.

The three major parties entered negotiations with very different visions of the future political system. The NP initially hoped for a system based on power-sharing among groups, coupled with the protection of the rights of each group to its "own community life," in keeping with ideas first set forth in 1986.[24] The NP was soon forced to abandon its original idea of group representation, which the ANC rejected as a thinly disguised form of apartheid, and started advocating instead a decentralized federal system with a weak center, hoping that this could become a vehicle for the protection of group rights. The ANC favored a unitary state with three levels of government that would provide strong protection for individual rights but no space for anything that could turn into group representation. Inkatha wanted a highly decentralized federal system, almost a confederation. Its main goal was an autonomous KwaZulu/Natal region, virtually a republic in which Zulus would be the "constituent nationality." Inkatha's vision thus contained a strong element of ethnic representation.

The Constitution of the Republic of South Africa (the interim constitution) was adopted on December 22, 1993. A compromise between the ANC and NP positions, it left many issues deliberately ambiguous. Three areas were particularly important in this respect: the bill of rights, the organization of the provinces, and the issue of traditional authorities.

The bill of rights (Chapter 3 of the constitution entitled "Fundamental Rights") enumerated a long list of individual rights and liberties.

The only articles in this chapter touching upon group rights dealt with language and education. Article 31 recognized every person's right to participate in the cultural life of his or her choice—meaning that any group could organize a cultural organization to reflect its identity and aspirations but could not keep anybody from joining it. Article 32 similarly gave every person the right to establish educational institutions based on common culture, language, and religion, but specified that these institutions could not discriminate on the ground of race. Thus, in all these provisions, the recognition of the right of people to maintain their culture and language was contradicted by the determination to make it impossible for whites to maintain segregated institutions, particularly schools.

Schedule 4 of the constitution, which outlined the basic principles that any future constitution was supposed to respect, contained similar contradictions. Article XII stated: "Collective rights of self-determination in forming, joining and maintaining organs of civil society, including linguistic, cultural and religious associations, shall, on the basis of non-discrimination and free association, be recognized and protected." The existence of collective rights was thus recognized and the very touchy issue of self-determination for presumably ethnic groups was raised. Then, both were modified through the provision against discrimination. In the end, the article simultaneously recognized and denied the right to self-determination.

The second area where compromise was reached by sacrificing clarity concerned the provinces, which were neither states in a federal system nor administrative subdivisions in a unitary one, but a little of each. The interim constitution created nine provinces, up from four in the old South Africa. The criteria used to demarcate these areas hinged primarily on economic viability and administrative efficiency, but also included "historical boundaries" and "language and cultural realities." The commission established to draw up the provincial boundaries admitted that the latter criteria opened difficult problems, and that it would be dangerous to attempt to gerrymander the regions for the sake of language homogeneity:

> The reorganization of homogeneous language and cultural regions may provide the opportunity for the exploitation of ethnic sentiments, claims and counterclaims, and constant new majorities and minorities. On the other

hand, regional boundaries should not cut across the spontaneously formed areas where particular language communities live.[25]

The demarcation of the provinces gave rise to considerable disagreement: "There are very strong views in the country concerning land and borders and it would be an error to underestimate these emotions," concluded a commission member who thought the demarcation had been dangerously hasty.[26] Indeed, the interim constitution contained a list of problem areas where the issue of demarcation had proved so controversial that the location of the border would be submitted to a referendum after the elections.

The third area of ambiguity affecting ethnic conflict concerned traditional leaders. The apartheid system had given such leaders an official position in the administration of the homelands, although redefining their powers and goals to suit its purposes. The new constitution recognized traditional leaders, a decision fully supported by Nelson Mandela and the moderates in the ANC, but very controversial with more radical and younger members. Where traditional institutions still existed, Chapter 11 of the constitution stated, provincial legislatures were required to form a House of Traditional Leaders to advise "in respect of matters relating to traditional authorities, indigenous law, or the traditions and customs of traditional communities." Article XIII of Schedule 4 on constitutional principles also specified that the "institution, status and role of traditional leadership" was recognized by the constitution. Such statements were quite vague but not unimportant. Any recognition of traditional leaders was de facto also a recognition of ethnic groups and subgroups—since chiefs exercised their authority over such groups.

According to the formal political transition process, the task of defining more clearly the character of the new political system, eliminating contradictions and ambiguities, fell to the constituent assembly to be formed after the elections of April 1994.[27] In actuality, a start on this definition had been made even earlier, as the result of the political maneuvering among the major parties. The effect of this maneuvering appeared to be the strengthening of the autonomy of the Natal region, of which KwaZulu had become the dominant part, and thus in the long run of the other provinces.[28]

Two important developments affecting democracy and ethnic conflict took place in early 1994. One was the collapse of the Freedom

Alliance, the front of ethnic nationalist organizations that had come together to try to stop the transition process designed by the NP and the ANC. The other was the continued refusal by Inkatha to participate in the election. This refusal led to mounting violence between ANC and Inkatha supporters in KwaZulu and around Johannesburg, creating fears that the voting would lead to chaos. The Freedom Alliance collapsed because the differences among its members were much deeper than the common opposition to the transition. The collapse was precipitated by a revolt against Mangope in Bophuthatswana, which prompted members of Afrikaner nationalist organizations in the Freedom Alliance to intervene on his behalf. Instead of being greeted as saviors by Mangope's supporters, as they expected, the Afrikaners were met with violence. No matter how divided they might be among themselves, the inhabitants of Bophuthatswana did not want white extremists to interfere. The fall of Mangope marked the collapse of the nationalist opposition in Bophuthatswana. Shortly thereafter, the Ciskei leadership gave up as well.

The resistance by Inkatha continued, however, leading to an escalation of violence. This eventually prompted the NP and the ANC to make a last minute attempt to convince Buthelezi to allow Inkatha to take part in the elections. An agreement was reached. Inkatha submitted its candidates' lists and won a majority of the votes in Natal province, thus gaining control of the provincial legislature and representation in the cabinet. Buthelezi was offered the position of home affairs minister.

When the agreement was reached, it was believed that Buthelezi had been swayed by a guarantee that Zulu King Goodwill Zwelithini would be formally recognized as a constitutional monarch with a largely ceremonial role. A month later, it transpired that the king had received much more, namely millions of acres of state land, equivalent to about one-third of the region. Registered in his name, this land was supposed to be used by him for the good of the Zulus. The ANC apparently had not been aware of this deal, made by the NP-controlled government and Buthelezi.[29]

This land transfer had sweeping implications for democracy and ethnic relations in South Africa. It put enormous patronage, and thus power, in the hands of nonelected leaders—the king and the KwaZulu chiefs. It weakened the position of other organizations that had no similar sources of patronage. To obtain land to cultivate or on which to build a house, people would have to turn to the king and the chiefs, not to the market or the civil servants operating under rules of political neutrality. In a sense, the land transfer settled, by creating facts on the ground, questions that the constitution did not answer clearly about the autonomy of the provinces, the power of traditional authorities, and the recognition of group rights. While the deal affected only Natal directly, it was bound to have repercussions on other parts of the country.

. . . .

ETHIOPIA

■   THE ATTEMPT BY THE ETHIOPIAN GOVERNMENT to manage ethnic conflict carried the strong imprint of the old Soviet model, although the TPLF and EPRDF, the broader front the Tigreans controlled, appeared to have relinquished their Marxist-Leninist orientation upon coming to power. At least concerning the "problem of the nationalities," however, the Meles regime remained dogmatically and anachronistically attached to the Soviet approach. This orientation became clear in the discussions that accompanied the writing of a new constitution and even more clearly in the policies enacted after the 1992 elections. By following the Soviet lead, the Ethiopian government had embarked on a path bound to lead either to increased repression or to mounting ethnic conflict and the eventual disintegration of the country. That, at least, was the lesson of Yugoslavia and the Soviet Union itself.

The Soviet influence was evident in the government's national and regional policies. At the national level, the TPLF was determined to strengthen Tigrean hold on power. The perception was growing among non-Tigreans that the government was purging the ranks of the civil service, the parastatals, and the educational institutions of other ethnic groups. The purges were apparently conducted on the pretext of reducing public sector employment as part of a structural adjustment program supported by the World Bank, but the axe fell disproportionately on some ethnic groups. At the regional level, the government was trying to consolidate the ethnic identity of each area, promoting an ethnic leadership and ethnic institutions, though always under the umbrella of the Tigrean-controlled EPRDF.

Inevitably, the insistence that each region belonged to a specific group or groups led to friction both between and within regions. Boundary disputes arose immediately, particularly in the lowland areas where conflict among different pastoralist groups for control of pasture land was endemic. Oromos and Somalis in southeastern Ethiopia were particularly divided. Conflict between regions also became an obstacle to sharing economic resources for the country's overall development. The regions, which received only minimal financing from the bankrupt central government, were encouraged to raise their own revenue. With a very small tax base because of widespread poverty and with no tax-collecting apparatus in place, many provincial governments tried to raise money in the simplest possible way—taxing merchandise crossing the region's borders. The potential for conflict, as well as for great damage to an already depressed economy, was great.

The new policy also encouraged strife within the regions. Since each of them was identified with a constituent nationality, or in a few cases several constituent nationalities, other groups were at a disadvantage. Episodes of ethnic cleansing were reported, ranging from killings or expulsion of individuals of the "wrong" group from some villages, to attempts by Oromo students at Alemaya University near Harar to oust their colleagues belonging to different groups to make the university into an Oromo institution. Systematic documentation on these episodes is lacking, but anecdotal evidence suggests that the phenomenon was widespread.

The restructuring of Ethiopia along ethnic lines was an obstacle to democratization and human rights in other ways as well. The independent press, for example, found it increasingly difficult to distribute publications outside the capital city. The reason, the government explained, was that each nationality had the right to its own language, which would be violated by the distribution of Amharic-language publications in regions where the mother language was different. Language rights were twisted into a repressive instrument to limit freedom of speech and information.

In early fall of 1994, the new Ethiopian constitution was still being prepared, and there were no clear indications yet on how the government intended to handle the issues arising from the division of the country into ethnic areas. A preliminary document circulated for discussion was rather vague. The document, couched in the old Soviet terminology, recognized an absolute right of nationalities to self-determination and singled out as the only issue open for discussion whether self-determination also entailed the right of secession. What self-determination meant in the absence of secession was not clear, except for a very vague concept of freedom from "suppression."[30] Nor did the document touch upon the existence of minorities in all regions and raise the question of how they could be protected. The discussion remained very theoretical and failed to address concrete problems.

Actions were more enlightening than the constitutional discussion points. The government's actions suggested that it had no intention of allowing any nationality to secede but was determined to maintain firm control over the entire country. Independent ethnic movements, above all the OLF, were seen as enemies, and the groups affiliated with the EPRDF were promoted in their place. The government appeared thus to be following the old Soviet model not only in the theoretical approach, but also in the policies it implemented.

For their part, the major opposition groups did not appear to have viable ideas for solving the problem of ethnic relations. Of the major groups, Amharas remained opposed to the division of the country, seeing it as a plot against them. Like the Serbs in Yugoslavia, Amharas were present in all parts of the country and believed that unity rather than separation protected their interests. The Oromo Liberation Front, on the other hand, shared the Marxist-Leninist theoretical orientation of the TPLF concerning the problem of ethnic relations. It, too, argued for the right of nationalities to self-determination and the creation of ethnic regions. Nevertheless, the OLF rejected the system the TPLF was developing, claiming it did not represent genuine self-determination and was only a thin disguise for Tigrean domination. Concerned about Oromo rights, the OLF was oblivious to those of other groups. The southern part of the country, which the OLF considered to be "Oromia," was occupied by many small ethnic groups, not just by the Oromos. What the rights of these minorities were, and how they could be reconciled with those of the Oromos, were issues on which the OLF charter was silent. Oromo nationalism was thus a threat to other groups.

In June 1994, Ethiopia held elections for a constituent assembly. Presented by the government as another step toward the transformation of Ethiopia into a completely democratic country, free of both repression and ethnic conflict, the elections in reality promoted neither democracy nor ethnic peace. The major, independent political organizations did not participate in the elections. As in 1992, voters were not presented with real choices, although this was somewhat less obvious this time. Over half the registered candidates ran as independents, disguising their affiliation with the EPRDF-aligned parties. And increasingly bitter opposition groups, the OLF foremost, responded by threats of armed resistance. Unable to manage ethnic tensions, Ethiopia appeared headed for more conflict and repression, not for democracy.

. . . .

CONCLUSIONS

■   THE FAILURE TO ADDRESS THE PROBLEM of ethnic relations in a satisfactory way remains in 1994 a major source of conflict and an impediment to a democratic transition in all countries under discussion.

Underlying the failure is a mixture of political factors and inadequate institutions. The narrow nationalism of the governments of Slovakia and Croatia, the extremism of the Serbian minority in Croatia and its backers in Serbia, the determination of Buthelezi to raise the flag of Zulu nationalism in order to ensure for himself a power base in post-apartheid South Africa, the strategy of divide and rule used by the TPLF leaders in trying to govern an ethnically mobilized country where Tigreans are only a small minority, and the frustration of the Oromos who have failed to carve a political role commensurate with their numbers, are some of the political factors explaining why ethnic conflict remains a major problem in all four cases. In addition, the four countries also adopted constitutions and structured political institutions that worsened, or at least did little to lessen, the tensions among the various ethnic groups.

Ethiopia's approach was the least promising. It chose the model that had guided the Soviet Union, and also Yugoslavia and Czechoslovakia, in the past. The evidence from these countries shows that such systems can maintain unity and contain ethnic conflict only as long as the center remains strong and repressive. Disintegration results when the center weakens during a political opening. The system chosen condemned Ethiopia to continued authoritarianism or to disintegration. Ethiopia thus offers a lesson on how ethnic conflict should *not* be managed by countries pursuing democratization.

The other countries are far from finding a formula for managing ethnic conflict successfully. Their initial choices are more conducive to correction and reform, so problems could probably be better addressed by incremental changes, rather than a total revamping of the approach. The Croatian and Slovak constitutions and laws on minorities do recognize some special rights for members of minority groups, although they also contain highly discriminatory language. The agreement with Inkatha in South Africa did not settle the issue of ethnic group rights, but it did show the possibility of a compromise solution.

Part IV.
Managing Ethnic Conflicts in a
Democratic Process

INTRODUCTION

■ THE EXPERIENCE OF THE COUNTRIES under discussion shows that the demands of mobilized ethnic constituencies fall into two broad categories: the dual quests for equal rights and for a separate identity. The demands for equal rights were evident in the refusal of the minorities in Slovakia and Croatia to accept constitutions that differentiated between categories of citizens, and in the innumerable clauses in the South African constitution that aimed at preventing whites from maintaining their separateness and their privileged position. The demand for identity was evident in the refusal of the Hungarian minority in Slovakia or the Serbs in Croatia to be assimilated, or the demands of Afrikaner and Zulu nationalists in South Africa that they be given a separate homeland in which they could be autonomous. Demands for equality are satisfied in democratic systems by protecting individual rights. But individual rights are not seen as sufficient protection against assimilation and loss of identity by ethnic nationalists, who demand protection and recognition for groups.

The tension between individual rights and freedoms and the collective rights demanded by ethnic constituencies lies at the heart of the conundrum of democratization in multi-ethnic societies. Democracy requires protection of individual rights and freedom of choice for each citizen. Ethnic nationalism introduces a set of collective demands. The emphasis on the collectivity rather than the individual is a characteristic of authoritarian, not of democratic regimes. Thus, the nationalistic explosions that accompany political openings risk destroying the possibility of a democratic transition. Indeed, many writers, particularly in Eastern Europe, have argued that nationalism shares many common characteristics with communism and that this explains the ease with which former communist officials have turned to nationalism.

Establishing a balance between individual and group rights requires the political will to accept compromise by the major parties to the conflict. The actual crafting of a workable solution, however, can be greatly facilitated by the existence of a body of established principles and a set of institutional models that enjoy widespread support, not only in the specific country, but also in the broader international community. An agreement is easier when the negotiating parties do not have to reinvent the wheel.

While there is no indication that European and African countries differ in terms of the political will to compromise, Europe has a substantial advantage when it comes to the existence of common principles and models to guide democratization in multi-ethnic societies. Western Europe has elaborated over the years a set of concepts and institutional models to reconcile democracy and ethnic demands. These ideas have an influence on post-communist regimes anxious to see their countries accepted as an integral part of Europe. Africa has not yet developed its own models and principles and European models have little attraction. They probably also have limited applicability.

A long history of conflict in Europe has forced governments there to accept the inevitability of ethnic nationalism and thus to devise solutions. African countries remain defensive about ethnic conflict and reluctant to accept that they cannot simply legislate it out of existence. Nevertheless, in all of them ethnicity influences politics, and most leaders do not hesitate to rely on ethnic allegiances to stay in power.

This defensiveness about ethnic conflict is an understandable reaction to the racism of colonial administrators and writers that looked down on African societies as being "tribal," thus underdeveloped and premodern. Today's "tribal" identities, furthermore, are not necessarily rooted in a distant past. They have been deeply affected, deliberately manipulated, or even created during the colonial period. The Zulu "tribe" is a case in point: it did not exist before Shaka conquered his empire, when the Zulus were an obscure Nguni clan, or in the days of the empire, which in any case only comprised the section of today's KwaZulu north of the Tugela River. Indeed, the Zulu tribe as defined by white South Africans only emerged after the Zulu empire was destroyed.[31] But African countries are not unique in this respect. In Europe, too, national identities are relatively recent, and history has been and is being rewritten all the time in support of modern claims and aspirations. The ironic result of the African defensiveness is that at a time commentators talk openly about a revival of tribalism in Europe, African governments continue to deny that ethnic identities are a permanent feature of all countries, and thus that they have to be dealt with. Having rejected the concept of "tribalism" as a colonial creation, Africans remain reluctant to accept ethnic nationalism as a universal phenomenon, which reappears in waves throughout the world.

. . . .

SELF-DETERMINATION REVISITED

■   IN A DISCUSSION OF PRINCIPLES AND CONCEPTS concerning ethnic nationalism, the idea of self-determination is central. Ethnic movements all over the world invoke the right to self-determination to justify their position. Unfortunately, there is little agreement about the meaning of self-determination. A general principle about the right of people to control their own destiny, self-determination leaves unanswered many fundamental questions. The most basic are: Who are the "people" entitled to control their destiny? And how may a people exercise self-determination? Is a separate state or regional autonomy required, or simply the right to participate in democratic political activity as an individual? Depending on how these questions are answered, self-determination can lead either to authoritarian nationalism or pluralist democracy.[32] The idea of self-determination contains within itself the conflict between democratization and nationalism experienced by multi-ethnic societies undergoing a political opening.

In practice, the meaning of self-determination has been constantly reinterpreted depending on historical circumstances. In the period immediately after World War I, when President Woodrow Wilson pushed the principle of self-determination onto the international agenda, the central political issue was the reorganization of Europe following the collapse of the Austro-Hungarian and Ottoman empires, and self-determination was interpreted mostly as statehood for "nations." In reality, it soon became clear that creating viable states and maintaining peace required considerable compromise and finessing, because there was no possible way of accommodating every population that could claim a distinct ethnic or linguistic identity into a separate state.

The minorities for which statehood was not a viable option were to be protected not only by the formation of democratic systems in which individual rights were recognized, but also by the recognition of their special rights as groups. The League of Nations established a system of minority treaties that guaranteed its protection to minority groups. This was a recognition that respect for individual rights did not constitute sufficient protection against both discrimination and forced assimilation but that the rights of the group as a whole also must be recognized and protected.[33]

After World War II, the idea of self-determination was reinterpreted by the United Nations in a much more restrictive fashion, namely, as the right of colonized people to independence. The revulsion against the extreme nationalism of nazism and fascism, the freezing of the new borders of Eastern Europe and the Balkans by the Soviets, and the dismantling of the colonial empires all contributed to this narrow interpretation of self-determination as decolonization, and thus to the delegitimization of the collective claims of national minorities.

Decolonization led to the formation of a large number of new states, all jealous of their newly acquired independence and sovereignty, and little inclined to take into consideration minority claims threatening the integrity of the state or even limiting the power of the central government. This contributed to the narrow interpretation of self-determination as decolonization, particularly since most of the new states were authoritarian and thus not inclined to interpret the concept to mean the right of individuals to participate in a democratic process.

In contrast to the League of Nations, the United Nations did not see the issues concerning minorities to be related to self-determination. Since many member states feared that dealing with minority issues would encourage separatist movements, the United Nations proved extremely reluctant to do so. No article on minorities was included in the Universal Declaration of Human Rights, and for over four decades the organization continued to avoid the question of group rights.[34] Indeed, it was only in 1992, when the problems of ethnic conflict could no longer be ignored, that the United Nations adopted an instrument devoted exclusively to the issue of minority rights, the Declaration on the Rights of Persons Belonging to National or Ethnic, Religious or Linguistic Minorities.[35]

REVIVING THE CONCEPT OF GROUP RIGHTS

■ THE COLLAPSE OF THE SOVIET EMPIRE, like that of the Austro-Hungarian and Ottoman empires, forced a reexamination of the idea of self-determination. It also revived the clash between the concept of self-determination as democracy and self-determination as nationalism.

Western countries hoped that populations freed from the control of communist regimes would opt for democracy as the means of controlling their destinies and realizing their aspirations. The Clinton administration in particular made democratization into one of its major foreign policy goals. For many groups and individuals, the desire for democracy was real. For others, the end of the old authoritarian regimes meant first and foremost the opportunity to pursue the nationalist goals suppressed by almost half a century of *pax sovietica*.

There is no way of assessing how many in each country thought of self-determination as democracy and how many as nationalism. Numbers were, in any case, less important than resolve and militancy. This was shown in the case of Slovakia, where the leaders' will to secede from Czechoslovakia prevailed over the public sentiment that opposed the move. And when it came to militancy, nationalists had the advantage— extremism is by definition not a characteristic of democrats.

The urgency of the nationalist demands and conflicts revived the debates concerning group rights and the protection of minorities within European institutions. Clearly, individual rights neither provided beleaguered national minorities with sufficient safeguard against discrimination and persecution nor satisfied their demand that their separate identity be recognized and protected against assimilation.

Africa's experience paralleled that of the former socialist countries, with the demand for greater democracy intertwined with ethnic claims. In most African countries, however, ethnic demands were less explicit than in Europe. Movements existed—such as in Ethiopia and South Africa—with openly nationalist goals and territorial revendications. Far more numerous movements appealed to ethnic sentiments but did not have an openly ethnic agenda. Most political parties formed in countries making the transition to multi-party systems, for example, fell into the latter category: they drew on ethnic support to gain power but never set forth a platform of ethnic demands.

Because of the more covert nature of ethnic nationalism in many countries, Africans were not forced to recognize its pervasiveness with the same clarity as Europeans. Even open, tragic outbreaks of ethnic conflict in Burundi in October 1993 and in Rwanda a few months later did not change attitudes. On the contrary, many Africans and Africanists tried to explain away the obvious ethnic components of the conflicts, stressing instead all the other factors that undoubtedly contributed to the violence. As a result, African governments and organizations continued to perceive ethnicity as something to be repressed. Whether it could be accepted and managed in a way that did not compromise democracy was not asked. Despite all the crises, there remained in Africa a real fear that recognizing the legitimacy of ethnic demands would simply encourage conflict and secession. As a result, countries like South Africa or Ethiopia, where ethnic nationalism was too overt to be ignored, have fewer guidelines and less support in trying to find a solution.

· ·

EUROPE: FROM SELF-DETERMINATION TO MINORITY RIGHTS

■ THE ORGANIZATIONS THAT HAVE BEEN MOST ACTIVE in recent years in developing principles to guide the management of ethnic conflict are the CSCE and the Council of Europe. The crises of the early 1990s prompted both organizations to look not only at principles concerning group rights and the protection of minorities but also at the concrete measures through which the principles need to be implemented.

The Helsinki Final Act of 1975, the CSCE founding document, was devoted mostly to relations among states, with the goal of improving security and enhancing cooperation among them. Only two articles dealt explicitly with the problem of how states should treat their citizens, that is, with the problem of human rights which became the focus of much of the CSCE activity. Article VII committed the participating states to respect the human rights and fundamental freedoms of individuals and to extend them to members of national minorities. Article VIII raised the problem of group rights. It upheld "the principle of equal rights and self-determination of peoples," and stated that all peoples have the right to determine "their internal and external political status." The problem of what constituted a "people" and how self-determination could realistically be exercised in multi-ethnic states was not defined.[36] However, it is clear that self-determination in the European context could not mean decolonization, but that it must apply to minorities, with all the resulting complications.

Only after the break-up of the Soviet Union did the CSCE have to confront squarely the ambiguities of the idea of self-determination. This led to a plethora of meetings and documents concerning what in the CSCE jargon is known as "the human dimension." As a result of this activity, the vague concept of self-determination of peoples, with its implicit challenge to the existing states, disappeared from the CSCE documents. It was replaced by much more precise principles concerning the rights of minorities and the protection to which they are entitled. If implemented, these principles would also protect existing states against the threat of secession.

Two CSCE meetings concerning the human dimension are particularly important for this study: the Copenhagen Meeting of the Conference on the Human Dimension of the CSCE, held in June 1990, and the Geneva Meeting of Experts on National Minorities, which took place in January 1991.

The document issued at the Copenhagen meeting contained a substantial section devoted to the problem of national minorities, declaring unequivocally that "questions relating to national minorities can only be satisfactorily resolved in a democratic political framework."[37] Democracy, not nationalism, was the answer to the problem. This document also implicitly recognized that minorities needed two kinds of protection: against discrimination and against assimilation. The protection against discrimination was provided by the respect of the rights of all individuals, including members of minority groups.[38] But protection against assimilation was more complex. The document recognized that protecting the ethnic, linguistic, cultural, and religious rights of minorities required more than safeguarding individual freedoms but had to be furthered "by establishing, as one of the possible means to achieve these aims, appropriate local or autonomous administrations . . . ."[39]

The report of the Meeting of Experts on National Minorities held in Geneva in January 1991 expanded on these ideas. It reiterated that democracy and the safeguard of individual rights were vital for the protection of national minorities, but it also recognized the additional need to protect collective rights. For example, members of national minorities had the same political rights as all other citizens, but also the right to be represented as minorities. Similarly, the experts stressed that all issues concerning minorities had to be settled through negotiations and consultations between the government and the representatives of the minorities seen as a collectivity.[40] The document also reiterated that the CSCE stood against the forced assimilation of minorities.

In July 1992, a summit of the heads of state or government of the CSCE countries reached the decision to establish a High Commissioner on National Minorities. The main task of the commissioner was to provide "early warning" of tensions involving national minorities that had "the potential to develop into a conflict within the CSCE area . . . ."[41] Clearly, the problem of minorities had become a central concern for the CSCE, both from the point of view of the human dimension and from that of international security.

Like the CSCE, the Council of Europe also responded to the increase in ethnic conflict in Eastern Europe by going beyond general and vague principles such as self-determination, developing instead guidelines on very specific issues. Several important documents were adopted in this period, including a European Convention for the Protection of Minorities, approved in February 1991, and a European Charter for Regional and Minority Languages, adopted in 1992. These charters will not be examined here in detail, because the ideas they contained are very similar to those elaborated by the CSCE. This similarity confirmed that a consensus had emerged in Europe on how to handle ethnic conflict in a democratic manner.

The violent ethnic conflicts that continue unabated in the former Yugoslavia, particularly in Bosnia but also in Croatia, raise questions about the significance of these documents. Did European institutions, unable to act decisively to stem the violence and the abuses, simply spend their time and efforts elaborating principles nobody had the political will to enforce? The answer is more complex. All the meetings and discussions did not stop gross violations of individual and group rights from occurring. While experts talked, ethnic cleansing was taking place in Bosnia, and Serbian houses were blown up in Croatia. Whether international institutions should intervene with force under such circumstances to stop the conflicts remains an open and troubling question.

Nevertheless, the discussions and documents pertaining to ethnic conflict and its management in a democratic framework should not be dismissed as useless. The existence of a common set of principles agreed upon by international organizations can help moderates to craft a compromise before a conflict reaches the acute phase. It can also offer ideas to guide the more radical parties in negotiating a solution after they reach a stalemate and accept that they cannot win an outright victory by force. Although in the fall of 1994 it is still too early to reach a definite conclusion, there are indications that both the Slovak government and the Hungarian minority look to CSCE and Council of Europe principles for guidance on how to reconcile their positions and prevent the escalation of conflict. Even in the much more difficult case of Croatia, where the Krajina has de facto seceded with Serbian backing, the principles set forth by the European organizations point to the measures to protect the Serbian minority that have to be taken to make reintegration even conceivable. For these reasons, all the documents discussed here are quite significant.

The problem of ethnic conflict and the rights of minorities is also being addressed in many European countries through specific initiatives directed at promoting negotiations and reconciliation in areas where ethnic tensions are high. The range of these initiatives is wide indeed, from sending CSCE observers to Kosovo and a small contingent of U.S. troops to Macedonia, to the numerous projects started by nongovernmental organizations (NGOs) working with local communities and local governments to open up a dialogue between aggrieved minorities and suspicious dominant groups. It is very difficult to reach any overall conclusion about the success of these initiatives. Nevertheless, they do point to the variety of outside interventions needed to help make political openings in multi-ethnic societies a first step toward democracy, instead of a first step toward increased ethnic conflict and possibly disintegration. They include not just diplomatic pressure, but in extreme cases even the use of force; and not just conflict-resolution efforts by foreign governments dealing with the top leadership, but also small scale mediation in local conflicts by NGOs.

. . . .

AFRICA: DEFENDING THE STATE

■   IN CONTRAST TO EUROPE, AFRICAN LEADERS and institutions were much slower to react to the increase in ethnic conflict that accompanied the political openings in many countries. In Africa and among Africanists, a great deal of defensiveness about ethnic conflict persists. Nobody writing about Bosnia denies that ethnic conflict is the main problem: yet, many analysts still feel compelled to disprove the ethnic roots of the violence in South Africa.

The principles governing Africa in the post-independence period were inevitably determined by the political problems of the moment. African leaders were conscious of the dangers posed by the fragile unity and weak sense of common identity in their newly independent countries when they created the Organization of African Unity (OAU) and established the principles to govern relations among African states.

The new countries were also very concerned about the problem of national sovereignty, thus more inclined to worry about the state than about its citizens. The result was twofold. In their relations with each other, African countries upheld the principle that colonial borders should be respected. In their relations with their citizens, the new governments denied them the right freely to organize politically, claiming that multiparty systems would turn into breeding grounds for ethnic conflict.

Adopted by the OAU in 1964, the principle of the sanctity of colonial borders required all governments to renounce demands for border changes, including those based on the ethnic identity of the inhabitants of particular areas. The preference of the people involved—their right to self-determination—was not an issue the state-centered OAU charter took into consideration.

The principle was respected with surprisingly few exceptions, because all governments shared a common interest in territorial integrity. It was challenged openly only by Biafra in its unsuccessful attempt to secede from Nigeria in 1967–1970, and by Somalia in its also unsuccessful attempt to annex the Ogaden region of Ethiopia in 1977–78. The only African country to gain its independence through secession, Eritrea, did not challenge the OAU principle but deliberately based its claims on it: Eritrea should be an independent country because it had been an Italian colony separate from Ethiopia, argued the nationalists.

The claim that multi-party systems would threaten the unity of African countries was made by most African leaders in the 1960s. It is still voiced today, most notably by President Yoweri Museveni of Uganda. The leaders argued that African parties would be inevitably based on ethnicity rather than ideology and thus would split the country apart. To be sure, fear of ethnic conflict was not the only reason for rejecting democratic systems—many leaders simply did not want competition. But the claim that multi-party systems strengthen ethnic identities also has some empirical foundation: most pre-independence movements had a strong ethnic base, and so do the parties that have emerged in the 1990s in countries holding competitive elections.

One country that could not simply bury ethnicity in a single-party system was Nigeria. With a large population, very diverse in ethnicity and religion, and a history of conflict among regions that went back to the early colonial period, Nigeria was forced to address the problem directly, but failed to do so without resorting to authoritarian solutions. The first Nigerian federation was characterized by strong regions and a relatively weak center, but also by a lopsided distribution of power among the regions. A series of reorganizations—the first was one of the triggering factors in the series of events leading to the secession of Biafra and the civil war—led to the formation of 12 states in 1967, 19 states in 1976, 21 states in 1987 and 30 in 1991. The multiplication of the states was an attempt to dilute the power of the major ethnic groups, while at the same time providing some space for the smaller groups and allaying their fear of domination. The constant reorganization of the states shows that Nigeria has never succeeded in creating a balance, although it has avoided another major, open crisis similar to the secession of Biafra.

Parallel to the territorial reorganization into ever smaller states other changes were taking place in Nigeria. First, the central government fell into the hands of the military, except during 1979–1983. Second, the power of the central government increased vis-à-vis the power of the states, which became almost completely dependent on federal largesse for their revenue due to the oil boom. The system thus became more centralized. Finally, free political activity was curtailed, with the military repeatedly banning political parties, allowing new parties to form only as long as they had no ethnic or regional ties, banning them again, forcing the emergence of a two-party system, and so on. Almost 30 years after experimentation began, Nigeria was no closer to finding a democratic solution to the problem of governing the complex multi-ethnic and multi-religious country than it had been in the early years of independence.

The desire to protect the territorial integrity of the state and the power of incumbent leaders contributed to the neglect of the human rights issue. The OAU was designed to defend existing states and help new ones come into existence through the self-determination of still colonized people. Consequently, it spent little time discussing the rights of African citizens, either individually or in groups. It was only in the late 1970s that the organization finally decided that it was time to elaborate an African document on human rights. The result was the adoption in 1981 of the African Charter on Human and People's Rights, also known as the Banjul Charter.

The document had some very interesting features. Although it recognized the importance of both individual and group rights, it did not define "groups" clearly, nor did it explicitly recognize the rights of ethnic or religious minorities, except as individuals. Instead, it set forth a vague concept of collective rights based, it was claimed, on the special culture of Africa, which stressed the community over the individual. But the only group the charter specifically mentioned was the family.

The charter also recognized that all peoples "shall have the unquestionable and inalienable right to self-determination" (Article 20). But the rest of that article, and even more unambiguously the discussions that took place before the charter was adopted, made clear that the right to self-determination applied only to peoples living under colonial domination or under white rule in South Africa and Namibia. Faced with the question whether self-determination authorized secession, "[t]he ministerial conference reviewing the draft charter were adamant that this was certainly not the case."[42]

Another unique feature of the charter was that it not only listed the rights but also the duties of the citizen "towards his family and society, the State and other legally recognized communities and the international community" (Article 27). Specifically listed were the duty not to compromise the security of the state, to strengthen national solidarity, and to preserve the territorial integrity of the state (Article 29). In other words, the only subnational entity specifically mentioned was the family— a politically safe group that does not challenge the territorial integrity of the state. On the other hand, so strong was the emphasis on national solidarity that the charter recognized that in its name individuals could be forced to join associations, an exception to the principle of free association otherwise endorsed in the document (Article 10.2). Like the OAU charter, the African Charter on Human and People's Rights remained very defensive of the state. The issue of minorities was not considered.

The Banjul Charter was signed in 1981, although it did not come into force until 1986. The states signing the document were, with few exceptions, dominated by authoritarian regimes. Although ethnicity affected politics everywhere, it did not have to be acknowledged under such conditions. By the early 1990s, the situation had changed drastically. A political opening had taken place in many countries, and ruling parties were being forced to allow opposition movements to form. As Africa's founding fathers had predicted, most of these new organizations had an ethnic rather than ideological base. Ethnic demands and conflict increased everywhere. Contrary to what happened in Europe, however, African institutions did not take note of the new reality and remained unwilling to acknowledge that ethnic divisions were pervasive, inevitable, and that they could not be legislated out of existence.

The major initiative of this period was the attempt to create an African organization in the image of the CSCE. The idea for a Conference on Peace, Security, Stability, Development and Cooperation in Africa (CSSDCA) was launched by the African Leadership Forum of General Olusegun Obasanjo, the former Nigerian military leader who in 1979 had voluntarily stepped down, leading his country into a four-year interlude of civilian government. Since that time, Obasanjo has been a voice for reconciliation and democracy in Africa.

The initiative resulted in a large meeting in Kampala in May 1991, which was attended by a number of current and former African heads of state. Notable because it was an independent undertaking, the Kampala Forum also showed the difficulty of sustaining initiatives not dominated by governments or state-centric institutions like the OAU. One of the major decisions of the meeting was that the CSSDCA should be implemented within the OAU framework. The task of furthering the idea thus passed to the OAU bureaucracy.

The forum approved the Kampala Document—the equivalent of the Helsinki Final Act for the CSCE—which outlined the principles to be respected by all countries joining the CSSDCA. These principles were divided into four sections, known as "calabashes," namely security, stability, development, and cooperation. The stability calabash dealt with relations between African states and their citizens, thus raising specifically the issues of democracy, human rights, and ethnic conflict.

The principles contained in the stability calabash amounted to the acceptance of democracy and the rule of law. In a peculiar mixture of broad, general principles of democracy and very specific suggestions, the document stressed the need for government transparency and accountability, pluralistic political systems, and constitutions containing a bill of rights, but it also prescribed measures such as the adoption of a system of proportional representation.

Concerning ethnic issues, the Kampala document remained on the well-trodden African path. Although it stated that "every country would ensure that there is no hindrance to alternative ideas, institutions and leaders competing for public support," it also stressed that "political organizations should not be created on religious, ethnic, regional or racial basis or considerations . . . ." If applied, such a principle would lead to the outlawing of most political parties on the continent. It was thus a futile attempt to outlaw reality, rather than a realistic measure to cope with a problem. In the Kampala document, as in the Banjul charter, protection of the integrity of the existing state remained the paramount concern.

The Kampala document thus did not open new ground concerning the issue of ethnicity and its relations to democracy in African countries.

Instead, it reconfirmed the past trend of denying the legitimacy of ethnic identities in the political process and of trying to outlaw them.

. . . .

CONCLUSIONS

■　THE ETHNIC CONFLICTS THAT ACCOMPANIED the demise of socialist regimes in Europe and many authoritarian governments in Africa will not soon subside. They will remain a threat to democratization and, in the most extreme cases, to peace and to human life.

European institutions have faced the reality of ethnic conflict and have started to think of solutions that discourage secession and are compatible with democracy. African countries have not. In the past, fearing that democratization would enhance ethnic conflict, African leaders defended authoritarian solutions. Under pressure from their own populations and the international community, they found it increasingly difficult during the 1990s to maintain the authoritarian hold on power provided by single-party systems or no-party military regimes. They did not, however, admit that they could not open up their political systems without increasing the level of ethnic competition, and thus that they had to find ways to accommodate ethnic demands. Conferences, charters, and lofty principles by themselves do not provide solutions to ethnic conflict, as the continuing strife in Eastern Europe unfortunately shows. In Africa, the absence of a common framework of principles makes the solution even more elusive. The work remains to be done.

Part V.
The Challenge for the United States

INTRODUCTION

■ DEMOCRATIZATION AND ETHNIC CONFLICT have been closely associated in many parts of the world during the early 1990s. Democracy has emerged as the unchallenged ideology to prescribe how the business of politics should be conducted and governmental power exercised. In practice, however, democracy is being thwarted by the force of ethnic nationalism.

In an interesting historical parallel, the demise of the Soviet empire has unleashed a wave of nationalism similar to the one that followed the fall of the Ottoman and Austro-Hungarian empires in the early twentieth century. The map of Eastern Europe and Central Asia has changed drastically and will probably undergo other modifications before stabilizing. In Africa, the colonial empires disappeared earlier, but their territorial legacy lived on in the form of the colonial borders frozen in place after independence. This legacy of the colonial empires is also being called into question by the upsurge of ethnic nationalism.

To the United States, embarked on a carrot-and-stick program of encouraging and coercing authoritarian regimes to move toward democracy, ethnic nationalism is a considerable challenge. Stimulated by political openings, ethnic nationalism can halt further progress toward democracy and cause great violence and dramatic violations of human rights. As a result, in many countries, political openings have a perverse outcome. Socialism was a benign system in Bosnia, when compared to the chaos that replaced it. For the victims of ethnic violence in Burundi in late 1993, the authoritarianism of the military regime was less dangerous than the massacres that followed the installation of a democratically elected government.

The U.S. policy of encouraging democratization does not cause ethnic violence—as the cases discussed here indicate. The link between political openings and ethnic conflict is far more complex, and there is no simple cause and effect relation. Nevertheless, any political opening clearly creates space for ethnic nationalism to flourish. As a result, the United States cannot ignore this problem in its efforts to promote democratization. In Burundi, a country subject to recurrent waves of ethnic conflict, the United States encouraged and supported the elections of June 1993 with funds, observers, and various democratization programs. The elections were won by a party representing the Hutu majority, which duly formed the new government, replacing the Tutsi-dominated military one. The incumbent president graciously stepped aside and was much feted in Washington for having done so. The military did not accept the results. There followed an attempted coup in October 1993 and a wave of ethnic killings. The full sequence of events was not preordained, but the victory of a Hutu party was predictable, and the possibility that the military would not accept the results, very strong.

The example of Burundi is a stark reminder of the dangers involved in promoting democratization in multi-ethnic countries, particularly those with a history of recurrent ethnic conflict. This does not mean that the United States should stop encouraging democracy. On the contrary, democracy offers the best hope for the management of ethnic conflicts, but only if the special requirements of multi-ethnic societies are taken into consideration.

. . . .

THE ISSUE OF GROUP RIGHTS

■ A DEMOCRATIC, MULTI-ETHNIC COUNTRY, the United States may paradoxically be ill prepared to deal with the problems of democracy in other multi-ethnic countries. In its own history, the United States has approached ethnic problems on the assumption that the best solution resides in strong protection of individual rights. This approach appeared to work in the 1960s, when the civil rights movement focused on the grossest aspects of discrimination and inequality. It is working less well in the 1990s, when some advocates for minority groups are arguing that individual rights are not sufficient to provide a meaningful political role for minorities, and that without sufficient political clout neither equality of rights nor recognition of cultural diversity can be ensured. The controversy that surrounded the Clinton administration's decision in May 1993 to nominate Lani Guinier to head the Justice Department's civil rights division is a good reminder that this is an extremely sensitive issue in the United States at present. Succinctly stated, Guinier argued in several law review articles that the protection of the individual right to vote did not provide blacks as a group with sufficient political representation. She also challenged the notion that simple majority rule was the only form of democracy, suggesting alternate mechanisms for ensuring that minorities acquire better representation. The speed with which her nomination was withdrawn when politicians became aware of her writings showed that the concept of group rights remains unacceptable in the mainstream of U.S. thinking. Yet, it is this issue of group rights that needs to be addressed by multi-ethnic countries undergoing a political transition.

Whether the United States will be able to continue to rely on the protection of the individual to solve its domestic ethnic problems, or whether it will be forced to reconsider group rights is still an open question. But multi-ethnic countries now experiencing a political opening simply cannot avoid tackling the issue of the collective rights of ethnic groups, as the cases discussed in this study show. For the Hungarian minority in Slovakia, fearful of both discrimination and forced assimilation, or for the Oromos in Ethiopia, feeling aggrieved by almost a century of domination by northerners, the burning issue is the position of the group. If the group does not have sufficient power, who can protect the individual rights of its members? The answer, that a democratic, accountable government would do just that, is meaningless to minorities, convinced that the government is not democratic and that, far from being accountable to all citizens, it is dominated by another ethnic group. Political reality, not democratic theory, forces these countries to deal with the controversial issue of the position of ethnic groups as groups in a democratic political system.

. . . .
EUROPE: FROM PRINCIPLES TO IMPLEMENTATION

■   EUROPEAN COUNTRIES AND INSTITUTIONS are explicitly dealing with this issue. This essay has reviewed the principles embodied in the documents of the CSCE and the Council of Europe in recent years. In addition, many Western European countries—Belgium, Holland, Switzerland, and Italy, for example—have developed over the years a variety of political mechanisms (which cannot be examined here) for managing ethnic conflict. All of these principles and mechanisms share one common goal: to enable different ethnic groups to maintain their identity and a degree of autonomy, while at the same time remain together in one country. From the point of view of the minorities, these systems provide protection and a degree of autonomy; from the point of view of the state, they prevent secession and disintegration.

There is thus no shortage of principles and models that could help Eastern European countries manage their ethnic conflicts. The real problem is implementation, and here lies the challenge for the United States in its efforts to promote democracy.

Two distinct categories of countries exist and require different policies. In the first category are countries such as Slovakia, where ethnic conflict lurks as a distinct possibility but has not erupted into violent confrontation. In such cases, the United States must take a strong position on the standards of inter-ethnic relations it expects the government and the leaders of minority groups to respect if the country is to continue to be recognized as democratizing and receive help on those terms. For example, the United States needs to make very clear that constitutions that discriminate against some categories of citizens are not acceptable in a democracy and that this will influence the allocation of aid and relations with the United States in general. Leaders of minorities also need to be put on notice that the United States does not consider secession a solution and that their demands will receive support only insofar as they conform to recognized principles about the rights of minorities. In other words, the United States needs to make explicit to all sides its intention to take seriously the principles contained in international documents.

The management of ethnic conflict in these countries does not just require agreement at the top. Ethnic relations are lived out in local communities, and it is often at this level that problems get out of control. Small-scale initiatives by nongovernmental organizations working to defuse ethnic tensions can be extremely valuable and deserve increased support.

The second category of countries includes those where ethnic conflict has led to civil war. Eventually, the solution here, too, can only be the formation of democratic governments structured to accommodate the rights of the minorities. But before such outcome becomes even remotely thinkable, the conflict must end. This means that the first task for the United States and other outsiders is to attempt to mediate the conflict. In extreme cases military intervention by the international community is the only policy that can have an impact on ethnic conflict. Whether the United States should consider military intervention is not a question that can answered in general terms. The answer depends on the specifics of each situation, what can realistically be achieved through intervention, and whether the political will to pay the political and human costs of intervention can be summoned. In extreme cases, however, the choice is not between military intervention and alternative steps, but between military intervention and inaction.

Partition is another issue that needs to be addressed in the case of war-torn countries. Partition is not a solution to ethnic conflict, because the new states are rarely homogeneous and the vicious circle starts anew. The United States should continue to oppose partition on principle. Nevertheless, there are situations that have deteriorated so badly that the disintegration of the country becomes inevitable—Yugoslavia in 1990 is an example. Even in these cases, new governments must be made to understand that the United States accepts partition not as the end of a process, but as the beginning of a solution to ethnic conflict. Thus, countries will receive support only to the extent they are working toward reconciliation and compromise. Intransigent, nationalist governments in new countries create a vicious circle of conflicting nationalisms and should not be supported.

. . . .
AFRICA: ESTABLISHING THE GROUND RULES

■   AFRICA PRESENTS A DIFFERENT CHALLENGE. There, open ethnic conflict is still rare, but leaders and institutions have not agreed on a common set of principles on how to handle ethnic pluralism in their societies; in fact, they have not even started discussing the issue seriously.

There still is an unrealistic official attitude that ethnic identities need to be suppressed or officially ignored, while unofficially most governments and opposition groups play the ethnic card to strengthen their position. This is nothing new. For the last 30 years, authoritarian regimes have condemned ethnic allegiances in public and manipulated them informally to keep themselves in power. Democratization requires different solutions. Accountable, transparent governments must rely on principles and visible institutions, not on covert deals and personal alliances.

The United States and other countries seeking to promote democracy in Africa need to help African institutions and individual governments devise a more realistic approach to ethnic conflict and, above all, one more compatible with democracy. The first task is to convince governments and institutions that the issue needs to be addressed. Pretending that political systems in multi-ethnic countries can be ethnic-blind can lead to a crisis similar to that of Burundi. Banning ethnic parties in countries where most parties have an ethnic base helps neither the cause of democracy nor that of ethnic peace. The second task is to help African countries devise solutions that suit their specific situations. The search for a workable approach to democracy in multi-ethnic African countries needs to go beyond the simple formulas of power-sharing and federalism that are often suggested lately. There are many ways of sharing power and many ways in which a unitary state can be transformed into a federal one. Not all would decrease ethnic tensions or be compatible with democracy.

An objection often raised against political systems that recognize a role for ethnic groups is that they encourage conflict rather than decrease it. From this point of view, if the United States put pressure on African countries and institutions to accommodate ethnic demands, it would simply be promoting conflict. Such an objection does not appear valid. Election after election shows that voters cast their ballots according to their ethnic or regional preferences; episodes of ethnic cleansing are numerous; even movements with openly secessionist goals are multiplying. The horse has already bolted, and it is too late to close the barn door.

Nevertheless, recognizing a legitimate political role for ethnic groups remains an extremely delicate problem. Depending on the circumstances, ethnic identities can be fairly fluid or quite rigid, salient or relatively unimportant. A political system that gives recognition to ethnicity undoubtedly encourages ethnic identities to be both rigid and salient. But ethnic conflict has the same effect, and at a much higher price. At present, the cost of admitting that political systems have to take ethnicity into account appears lower than the cost of pretending that ethnicity can be made to disappear.

The difficult question is not whether ethnic demands must be addressed, but how they can be met without creating worse problems or destroying democracy. That the answers are the same in Africa as in Europe should not be assumed. For example, the problem of ethnicity in most European countries is that of relations between a dominant group and minorities. Many African countries have no dominant group; the population is much more fragmented. The situation requires different solutions.

European institutions have also singled out the cultural and language rights of minorities as a salient issue. In Africa, language problems may be less important, and, in any case, may not lend themselves to the same solutions. European minorities fight for the right to use their mother tongue and have their children educated in it. The number of languages used in any one European country is limited, however, and most are also spoken in neighboring countries, giving their users access to existing bodies of written information. In Africa, the situation is much more confusing. Most languages were neither codified not written until the last few decades, making it much more difficult to distinguish between dialects and languages. The number of languages as a result is much greater— Nigeria alone is deemed to have some 400 of them. Mother tongue education under such conditions would cause nightmarish administrative problems, and perhaps not even satisfy a felt need of many ethnic groups. In Ethiopia, where the government is promoting own-language education, the idea has been greeted with suspicion by some of the smaller groups, which fear such a policy may only isolate their children and further limit their opportunities.

The idea of local self-government also presents different problems in many African countries. Local autonomy could lead to the enhancing of the role of so-called traditional authorities—the chiefs that were integrated into the colonial administration and the post-independence administrative systems. Local autonomy could thus become an obstacle to democracy by creating a conflict between different kinds of political systems. The position of the Zulu monarchy in South Africa is a case in point. A greater role for traditional authorities could also have implications for land-use patterns and development strategies by strengthening communal land tenure. Again, South Africa provides an example. This does not mean that local autonomy is wrong in Africa, that traditional authorities should not play a role, or that only centralized systems can work. It is simply a reminder that local autonomy in Africa has different implications than in Europe.

The principles and the policies to guide democracy in multi-ethnic African countries will have to be elaborated by Africans themselves, not transferred from the outside. Nevertheless, any country or international institution that makes promoting democracy in Africa its goal needs to push Africans to address the problem of ethnicity. Individual countries and, more important, African organizations need to be encouraged to do so. The CSSDCA initiative may offer an opportunity to promote the discussion of individual and group rights, and of democracy in multi-ethnic societies, in a more realistic and productive direction than the futile outlawing of ethnic parties.

Where ethnic conflict has already erupted into open warfare, as in Rwanda, the problem cannot wait for the elaborations of principles and charters. The most important task is to stop the killing, by supporting military intervention if necessary. Even in these cases, it may be time to try to go beyond an agreement between leaders and confront the issue of how a multi-ethnic society with such an experience of bloodshed can be organized to prevent a new cycle of violence in the future.

The United States is bound to have an impact on the ethnic politics of African countries even if it does not address the problem directly. In particular, the demonstration effect of U.S. policy in the Balkans should not be underestimated. The United States has come to accept the division of Bosnia into ethnic enclaves—a system of apartheid hopefully without the discrimination aspect. The situation there probably does not lend itself to other solutions, but this is certainly not true everywhere. If the United States does not take an active role in helping countries find other approaches, it risks sending the message that multi-ethnic countries cannot last.

························

CONCLUSIONS

■ DEMOCRATIZATION AND ETHNIC NATIONALISM have emerged as two aspects of the process of political transformation during the 1990s. While democratic institutions in the long run provide the best means for managing ethnic tensions, in the short run the initial political opening can encourage outbreaks of ethnic nationalism, which can bring democratization to a halt. For the United States, which has put the promotion of democracy high on its foreign agenda, the challenge is to help countries move from the short run of the initial political opening to the long run of stable democracy. The case studies discussed here suggest that this challenge may have to be met in different ways in Europe and Africa. In Europe, where the rules of the democratic game in multi-ethnic societies are well established, bridging the gap between the short and long run appears to require above all efforts at mediation and conflict resolution, to create the political will to implement the rules. In Africa, the first step toward long-run solutions is to convince governments that multi-ethnic countries require special approaches to democracy and to help them devise appropriate solutions. Neither in Europe nor in Africa, however, can the goal of promoting democracy and managing ethnic conflict be separated.

Notes

[1] Ted Robert Gurr, *Minorities at Risk* (Washington, DC: United States Institute of Peace Press, 1993), p. viii.

[2] Slovenia was a partial exception, in that it experienced a stronger drive for democratization as well as for national independence, but space does not allow a discussion of that special case here.

[3] Victor Zaslavsky, "Nationalism and Democratic Transition," in Stephen Graubard, ed., *Exit From Communism* (New Brunswick, NJ: Transaction Publishers, 1993), p. 106.

[4] Lenard J. Cohen, *Broken Bonds: The Disintegration of Yugoslavia* (Boulder, CO: Westview Press, 1993), p. 46.

[5] Juan J. Linz and Alfred Stepan, "Political Identities and Electoral Sequence: Spain, the Soviet Union and Yugoslavia," in Graubard, op. cit., pp. 123–140.

[6] National Democratic Institute for International Affairs and African-American Institute, *An Evaluation of the June 21, 1992 Elections in Ethiopia* (Washington, DC: National Democratic Institute for International Affairs, 1992).

[7] Gale Stokes, *The Walls Came Tumbling Down: The Collapse of Communism in Eastern Europe* (New York: Oxford University Press, 1993), p. 151.

[8] Vàclav Havel, *Summer Meditations* (New York: Vintage Books, 1992), pp. 21–59.

[9] Jiri Pehe, "The Referendum Controversy in Czechoslovakia," *RFE/RL Research Report*, Vol. 1, No. 43 (30 October 1992), p. 37.

[10] Jan Obrman, "Polls Reveal Gloomy Mood Among Slovaks," *RFE/RL Research Report*, Vol. 2, No. 19 (7 May 1993), p. 51.

[11] For a discussion of the political implication of the -term "minorities" in former socialist countries, see Project on Ethnic Relations, "Romanian-American Symposium on Inter-Ethnic Relations," Bucharest, 17–18 June 1991, especially p. 3.

[12] The Constitution of the Republic of Croatia, Part I, "Historical Foundations," issued December 1990.

[13] "Human Rights and Democratization in Croatia," report prepared by the Staff of the Commission on Security and Cooperation in Europe, Washington, DC, September 1993, p. 10.

[14] Ibid., p. 12.

[15] The Constitution of the Slovak Republic, issued by the National Council of the Slovak Republic, 3 September 1993.

[16] "The Address Delivered by Ivan Gasparovic, The President of the Slovak National Council, on the Occasion of the Solemn Signing of the Constitution of the Slovak Republic," 3 September 1992.

[17] "Human Rights and Democratization in Slovakia," report prepared by the Staff of the Commission on Security and Cooperation in Europe, Washington, DC, p. 9.

[18] Ibid., p. 11.

[19] See Therese Nelson, "Forced Out of Their Homes in Croatia," *The Christian Science Monitor*, 22 February 1994.

[20] Milan Dukić, "Legal and Democratic Measures Toward Durable Peace," mimeo., 1993.

[21] Sharon Fisher, "Meeting of Slovakia's Hungarians Causes Stir," *RFE–RL Research Report*, Vols. 3 and 4 (28 January 1994), pp. 42–47.

[22] General Assembly of Local Government Representatives, Mayors and Members of Parliament of South Slovakia, "Statement on the Constitutional Status of Hungarians," Komárno, Slovakia, 8 January 1994.

[23] Ibid.

[24] National Party, Federal Congress for Freedom and Stability, "Speeches by the Proposers and Seconders of Motions," Durban, South Africa, 12–13 August 1986.

[25] "Report of the Commission on the Demarcation/Delimitation of the SPRs," 31 July 1993, paragraph 4.2.

[26] Ann Bernstein, "The Commission on the Demarcation of Regions: A Plea for a More Democratic Approach on Regions" (Minority Opinion on the Report of the Commission on the Demarcation/Delimitation of the SPRs).

[27] In April, the voters elected members of the National Assembly and the provincial legislatures. The National Assembly was one of the two houses of parliament. Members of the second house, the Senate, were nominated by the elected provincial legislatures, with each province nominating 10 senators. The National Assembly and the Senate, sitting jointly, formed the Constitutional Assembly, charged with amending the interim constitution.

[28] Under the new constitution, all homelands were reincorporated into South Africa, and their boundaries erased. KwaZulu thus became part of the larger Natal region. Since Inkatha won the elections in Natal, more autonomy for Natal meant more power for Zulu nationalists.

[29] *The Washington Post*, 23 May 1994.

[30] The Transitional Government of Ethiopia, The Constitution Commission, "A Paper on Basic Constitutional Concepts," Addis Ababa, November 1993.

[31] See Shula Marks, "Patriotism, Patriarchy and Purity: Natal and the Politics of Zulu Ethnic Consciousness," in Leroy Vail, ed., *The Creation of Tribalism in South Africa* (London: James Currey, 1989), pp. 215–240.

[32] For discussion see Guyora Binder, "The Case for Self-Determination," *Stanford Journal of International Law* Vol. 29, No. 2 (Summer 1993).

[33] See Natan Lerner, *Group Rights and Discrimination in International Law* (Dordrecht, London, Boston: Martinus Nijhoff Publishers, 1990), Chapter 1.

[34] Ibid., pp. 14–17.

[35] Gudmundur Alfredsson and Danilo Türk, "International Mechanisms for the Monitoring and Protection of National Minority Rights: Their Advantages, Disadvantages and Interrelationship," in Aric Bloed et al. (eds.), Monitoring Human Rights in Europe (The Netherlands: Kluwer Academic Publishers, 1993), p. 172.

[36] Conference on Security and Cooperation in Europe, "Final Act: Helsinki, 1975," Articles VII and VIII.

[37] "Document of the Copenhagen Meeting of the Conference on the Human Dimension of the CSCE," Section IV, 30.

[38] Ibid., Section IV, pp. 30–34.

[39] Ibid., Section IV, p. 35.

[40] "Report of the CSCE Meeting of Experts on National Minorities" (Geneva: CSCE, July 1961), Section III.

[41] Council on Security and Cooperation in Europe, "CSCE High Commissioner on National Minorities," Helsinki Document 1992, No. 3.

[42] Gino J. Naldi, *The Organization of African Unity: An Analysis of Its Role* (London and New York: Mansell Publishers, 1989), p. 126.

About the Author

MARINA OTTAWAY is the Davidson Sommers Fellow at the Overseas Development Council and a visiting professor of African Studies in the School of Foreign Service, Georgetown University. She has lived and taught in Africa for many years and has written extensively on the Horn of Africa, particularly Ethiopia, and on Southern Africa. Her most recent publications include *South Africa: The Struggle for a New Order* (The Brookings Institution, 1993).

About the ODC

ODC fosters an understanding of how development relates to a much changed U.S. domestic and international policy agenda and helps shape the new course of global development cooperation.

ODC's programs focus on three main issues: the challenge of political and economic transitions and the reform of development assistance programs; the development dimensions of international responses to global problems; and the implications of development for U.S. economic security.

In pursuing these themes, ODC functions as:

■ *A center for policy analysis.* Bridging the worlds of ideas and actions, ODC translates the best academic research and analysis on selected issues of policy importance into information and recommendations for policymakers in the public and private sectors.

■ *A forum for the exchange of ideas.* ODC's conferences, seminars, workshops, and briefings bring together legislators, business executives, scholars, and representatives of international financial institutions and nongovernmental groups.

■ *A resource for public education.* Through its publications, meetings, testimony, lectures, and formal and informal networking, ODC makes timely, objective, nonpartisan information available to an audience that includes but reaches far beyond the Washington policymaking community.

ODC is a private, nonprofit organization funded by foundations, corporations, governments, and private individuals.

Stephen J. Friedman is the Chairman of the Overseas Development Council, and John W. Sewell is the Council's President.

Board of Directors

Overseas Development Council

SPECIAL PUBLICATIONS SUBSCRIPTION OFFERS

U.S.-Third World Policy Perspectives • Policy Essays • Policy Focus

Subscribe to ODC's 1994 publications series and you will receive an invaluable source of independent analyses of U.S.-Third World issues—economic, political, and social—at a savings of over 15 percent off the regular price.

ODC's **U.S.-Third World Policy Perspectives** series brings 6–9 different perspectives presenting creative new policy options or insights into the implications of existing policy. Policy Perspectives for 1994 include *Population and Development: Old Debates, New Conclusions* by Robert Cassen and contributors, and *Intricate Links: Democratization and Market Reforms in Latin America and Eastern Europe,* by Joan M. Nelson with contributing chapters from experts from both regions.

Policy Essays explore critical issues on the U.S.-Third World agenda in 80-120 succinct pages, offering concrete recommendations for action. This subscription will bring you the first six essays in 1994.

Essay topics will include economic lessons from East Asia, population and development policy, the multilateral development banks and private sector development, structural adjustment in Africa, sustainable agriculture, and income distribution after structural adjustment in Latin America, among others.

Brief and easy to read, each **Policy Focus** briefing paper provides background information and analysis on a current topic on the policy agenda. In 1994, 6–8 papers will cover issues such as the environment and international trade, poverty and gender, the global threat of AIDS, and U.S. policy toward the multilateral development banks, among others.

1994 SUBSCRIPTION OPTIONS*

U.S.-Third World Policy Perspectives	$35.00
Policy Essay	$65.00
Policy Focus	$20.00

* Subscribers will receive publications issued to date upon receipt of payment; other publications will be sent upon release. Book-rate postage is included.

All orders require prepayment. Visa and Mastercard orders accepted by phone or mail. Please send check or money order to:

O | D | C

Publication Orders
Overseas Development Council
1875 Connecticut Avenue, NW
Suite 1012-PE
Washington, DC 20009